"Drew's k... ...edge of marketing in general is very strong, especially online marketing. He has a great command of the broad array of cutting edge systems and software packages available and helped us know which ones maximize our results. Highly recommend him!"

Susie & Rodger Engelau, ActionCOACH

"As the son of one of the UK's top business coaches, Drew is able to leverage his substantial background involvement in the business coaching industry to serve his clients well. Drew is high-quality person and worth doing business with!"

Eric Dombach , The Coaches Coach

"Drew, thank you. This was not just marketing hype, there was practical thinking that I could put to work immediately. This is timely and valuable information..."

David Marsh, Shirlaws USA

"*I have been working with Drew for some time now and he has revolutionised the marketing of my business coaching services, particularly the online tactics. His knowledge of marketing tactics for business coaches is quite amazing and he explains it all very effectively. I am now able to generate coaching leads in my sleep – literally! He is a true professional, always happy to go the extra mile and I would strongly recommend his services...*"

John Standaloft, Membership Director at the International Institute of Coaches & MD at Standaloft Coaching

"*Before working with Drew I was doubtful about how he could actually help me. I get lots of phone calls and emails from companies offering a similar service. That all changed when we embarked on the marketing program. Drew provided expert* *knowledge in online and off-line lead generation strategies, gave me access to tried and tested marketing that really works for Coaches, Trainers & Consultants and I immediately saw in increase in the amount of leads I was able to generate. I've learnt allot from Drew in a short space of time and would recommend his services to anyone who wants to generate more leads.*"

Lorna Powe, SalesPartners Cape Town

"Drew Edwards (MD) is a talented and skilled marketer offering creative and specialist marketing solutions for Business Coaches to consistently generate relationship leads. Drew is easy to do business with and has a proven track record of finding potential business for you!"

Samantha Gallagher, Pathfinders Coaching

"Drew Edwards has been wonderful for my coaching business. Before working with him, I spent almost 100 hours trying to attract clients through a single speech at a conference. I didn't get one client. Now, even though I haven't been able to devote 100% of my time to my business, I have a strategic alliance that's sending me referrals, my website visits are up 53% from a year ago, and I'm getting more and more Linked in contacts that are signing up for my webinars and free materials. This has led to complementary coaching sessions, more confidence and more clients. Thank you, Drew!"

Stacy Adams , SJA Coaching, Holden, MA, U.S.A

"Drew Edwards recently championed our LinkedIn marketing campaign. Although we were initially sceptical this would produce any meaningful results, we were pleasantly surprised when we started to average several qualified leads each day. Drew definitely knows his stuff, and if you sell business to business, I would strongly recommend you consider his proven LinkedIn strategies for lead generation..."

Karl Bryan/Adrian Ulsh, No Results No Fee

"Drew is a real find – expert in marketing, including a vast array of knowledge of the latest online opportunities and methods – he's totally focused and committed to helping his clients get results, and very good at it – Drew's enthusiasm is infectious – and he's fun! You can't argue with that!"

Catherine Llewellyn, Inspiring Change

"My name is Manuel and I have been a Coach for four years. Drew has a way of clearly explaining topics and provides tons of information around marketing and client attraction for Coaches, Trainers and Consultants. I would happily recommend Drew to anyone who wants more information about growing their business."

Manuel Rodríguez, Ology Coaching

"My name is Rick Adams and I've been in business for 8 years now. Drew has taught me the importance of marketing as a separate, essential, ongoing component of a successful business. It needs to be budgeted for in terms of time and money and it needs to get done. As Drew has pointed out, it doesn't matter how good you are at what you do, you have to attract customers."

Rick Adams, The Growth Consultancy

"I've been in business since 2006... Drew has shared many aspects of marketing and client attraction. I've also enjoyed hearing things from the viewpoint other coaches who are in a similar situation to me. Drews content is very informative and I would

definitely recommend him to other Coaches, Trainers or Consultants who want to grow their businesses."

Carlo Triolo , SASK Business Coach

"I have been in business as a Coach and mentor for 7 years, though in the big corporate world beforehand I was effectively doing a lot of this internally within the organisation and with the people in my teams. The biggest thing I've taken from Drew, is that there is no "magic bullet or one solution to build a successful business – You have to be persistently firing on all cylinders. I would happily recommend Drew to any Coach, Trainer or Consultant who wanted to know more about client attraction and business growth"

Alex Dyce, Lennox Hamilton Ltd

"I started my business 3 years ago now and since then there have been many examples of lessons I have learnt from Drew that have helped my business. Such as the way he continuously gives away his knowledge freely. Including an e-mail where he shared a story about only having a certain amount of seconds per day, then they have gone... I guess I can be one of those procrastinators sometimes! I would of course always recommend Drew to other Coaches, Trainers and Consultants."

Alan Harding, Better Business International Pty Ltd

"I have been in business as a consultant for 9 years. The biggest lesson I have learned, and continue to learn, from Drews communications to me is that nothing will happen if I don't do anything! I have a relatively "busy" business with an "acceptable" income. However I know I can do much better. It is the continuing realisation that what I want will not happen if I don't do anything towards it. I have been too comfortable for too long, enjoying working with my current clients and thinking all is well, when in actual fact I am only 2-3 client resignations away from panic! Drew has moved me to take action (at long last). Yes, I would be prepared to recommend him to a non-competing coach."

Phil Pickford, Think Differently

"Drew has taught me to be relentless, how to implement multiple client attraction strategies rather than relying on one method, measure performance and be prepared to change the plan if it's not working. Drew has a great handle on digital client attraction strategies and tactics. I would be happy to recommend his services on that basis."

Peter Wilkinson, Peter Wilkinson Ltd

"I'm John and I've been in business for 2 years now. Drew has taught me how to be relentless in my pursuit of Clients and use Linkedin and emails as powerful marketing tools they work if done correctly. I'd definitely recommend Drew and I have *already done so to some of my colleagues that needed help getting Clients."*

John Douglas, Exclusive Leadership Academy

"I've been in the Consulting/Coaching business for 14 years... But only 8 years here in Aus! After some initial scepticism I am finding Drews material highly useful – I have all sorts of issues that he's helping with and would of course recommend him to others... You have to kiss a lot of frogs in this business but I think Drew is the real deal!"

Nicholas Sutton, The Firefox Group

"My name is Dr.R. Benton Ruth, I'm the CEO/Owner of 'INSPIRE Business Solutions' and I've been in business for over 38 years. Drew provides simple, yet profound insights into marketing that produce results when applied. I would recommend Drew without reservation... He has the knowledge and experience."

Dr.R. Benton Ruth, INSPIRE Business Solutions

"I have Drews statement "Your prospects DON'T want or need a Coach. They want RESULTS!" on my desk. It says it all for me. I would recommend Drew to any Coach who is interested in attracting more clients. Lead generation is a need for all of us."

Gary C. Bizzo, Bizzo Management Group

"I've been an independent business consultant, trainer and coach for over 35 years. Drew clearly breaks down the three only things that any Coach, Trainer or Consultant should be focusing on if they want to increase business profits. I would certainly recommend Drew to anyone who wants to know more about marketing, lead generation and business growth."

Chris Jensen, Chris Jensen Coaching

Secrets of The Maverick Marketer

How Any Coach, Trainer or Consultant can Attract A Rush Of Clients With Less Work and Fewer Headaches

Drew Edwards

Secrets of The Maverick Marketer

Copyright © 2016 Drew Edwards
www.eliteclientattraction.com

ISBN 978-1-912009-58-9

First published as 'Magnetic Marketing', ISBN 978-1-907308-35-2
in Great Britain in 2014 by Compass Publishing
www.compass-publishing.com

Set by The Book Refinery Ltd
www.thebookrefinery.com

Contents

Contents

Preface

If you're a Coach, Trainer or Consultant and you're frustrated at the money you're making and the amount you know you're missing out on... and don't yet know how or what you need to do to attract more clients, generate more revenue and take your business to the next level...

And you know that one key step in the right direction is going to be enough to make it all start happening for you... Then this is the most important and exciting book you could ever read.

Because the truth is... regardless of recession, 'the economy', or even the stiffest, toughest, most cutthroat competition... You can enjoy vastly higher profits than you're getting right now. What's more, *you can easily enjoy these higher profits with less work, fewer headaches and a lot less hassle.*

I know this is a bold claim, but it's one I stand behind 100% – in fact, everything you'll discover in this book has achieved just that for Coaches, Trainers and Consultants all over the world.

Nothing you'll read in this book is based on guesswork or theory. It's based on proven strategies that are getting results for some of the world's top performing Coaches, Trainers and Consultants even as we speak.

But before you read any further...

I want to put you off if I possibly can, because this might not be for you!

Why?

Because I'm asking you to make a modest investment in the future success and even survival of your Business. But more than that, more than the actual money, is the commitment I'm asking you to make.

And if you're not the kind of person that is will¬ing to invest in your Business... Then what follows isn't for you and reading it will just be a waste of your time.

What's more, this message is definitely NOT for you if:

1. You believe that this — or anything else, for that matter — is going to work for you without YOU putting ANY effort in. If you think that, then you're reading the wrong message and listening to the wrong person. Make no mistake about it, to grow a successful Coaching, Training or Consultancy business there will be a substantial amount of work involved. But trust me, it will be worth it!

I'm telling you now, right up front, if you take this next step, then you're letting yourself in for some serious hard work. Don't continue reading if that puts you off — *because that's exactly my intention.*

2. You're not serious about increasing the number of leads you generate each month, the number of clients you have and your business profits. The fact is, most Coaches, Trainers and Consultants DON'T generate the amount of leads that they should, but with just a few tweaks to your marketing you will see a dramatic increase in the number of prospects you're able to attract.

IF you're the kind of person I'm looking for, you will discover how local business Coaches, Trainers and Consultants have gone from struggling to get by... to becoming the leading players in their sector and in some cases leading players worldwide.

Obviously I cannot guarantee you the exact same results for your own business, a lot will depend on your resolve and willingness to actually implement the strategies you'll get to access in this book. You will only get anything out of this book if you actually put to work what you'll discover.

3. You're unwilling to change what you're currently doing for the better. The truth is, IF what you're doing now isn't getting

you the results you want, it never will. To get better results you need to start doing things differently...if you're not willing to do that, please don't bother wasting both our time because this really isn't for you.

So... if you're still with me, then it tells me you're serious about wanting a dramatic improvement in your Business and you're prepared to knuckle down and work up a good sweat so that it happens.

And it tells me you're exactly the kind of person I want joining me!

A question you might be asking yourself if this is the first time you've heard from me is *"Who Am I And How Can I Help You Grow as a Coach, Trainer or Consultant"*.

I'm Drew Edwards, leading marketing and client attraction expert for Coaches, Trainers and Consultants and for the best part of a decade, I've dedicated my time into finding out what the top performing Coaches, Trainers and Consultants in the world do differently from everybody else...

Why is it that some can become extraordinarily successful, and then at the same time, in the same market, selling what is pretty much the same service, you can have others who just struggle to get by and just can't seem to generate the income they want or attract the clients they need?

What's the difference that makes the difference?

What I've found is that high achievers aren't any more intelligent than everybody else, they don't have a better service, they're not even necessarily better at what they do... But the one thing they do have, is a working, reliable and predictable system for bringing in clients, generating leads and increasing profits.

I now spend my time sharing that exact system with Coaches, Trainers and Consultants all over the world, so you can get similar results and transform your business too.

My clients include some of the world's top performing Coaches, Trainers and Consultants on both sides of the Atlantic and every month, Coaches, Trainers and Consultants from all over the world, attend my online seminars, events and video training programs. Over 5 thousand of them receive my business growth tips via email on a daily basis.

If I were you, the question I'd be asking is;

"Is there a reason why so many of the world's top performing Coaches, Trainers and Consultants so regularly take Drew's advice and put it into practice in their businesses?"

Of course there is. And I can assure you it's NOT because of my age, charm or good looks.

No, it's because I get results. And in the marketing game, that's what counts. It's ALL that counts.

Now, the reason I'm sharing this with you is not to brag. It's so that you know, that when I say I'm sharing something powerful and prof¬itable with you, then it's worth your while taking notice.

When I first started working with Coaches, Trainers and Consultants, one of the things I became obsessed with was studying the attitudes of the really successful ones and comparing them to the attitudes of those who were struggling. On the surface, it looks like successful people are successful because they do things differently. But if you look beyond that, you can see that successful people are in fact successful because they think differently.

You see, your thoughts control your feelings, your feelings then control your actions and your actions control your results. So your attitude and the way you think are the root of whatever results you're getting in your business at the moment.

So how do the successful Coaches, Trainers and Consultants think differently from everybody else?

Well, one thing I've noticed about the Coaches, Trainers and Consultants who are struggling, is that they have a wealth of excuses as to why they're in the situation they are in. These excuses can come in many forms, but whichever way you look at it, they are still just excuses. Whether it's the state of the; economy, personal circumstances, lack of funds or lack of knowledge.

The list is endless and it's just excuse after excuse.

Now I'm not saying that those things are easy to overcome, but they are just part of running a business. And you have to accept that. It's your attitude towards them that makes the difference.

Successful Coaches, Trainers and Consultants have a very different way of viewing things. They face the same challenges and obstacles as everybody else, sometimes even bigger obstacles. But they think differently, and instead of accepting things the way they are and using these obstacles as excuses for why they are NOT flourishing. They do something about them...

You see the harsh reality is you can generate leads, sign clients and make money or you can make excuses, you can't do both!

And it really is that simple...

No one is saying that being a successful Coach, Trainer or Consultant is easy. If it were, everyone would be doing it, but you need a certain attitude if you want to be successful, and part of that attitude means letting go of your excuses, standing up and taking responsibility.

In this book, you'll get access to some of the secrets that the top performing Coaches, Trainers and Consultants have *kept hidden for years.*

Chapter 1
The 3 Big Threats To Your Coaching, Training Or Consultancy Business And How To Avoid Them

During my many years working with Coaches, Trainers and Consultants from across the world, I've noticed some major changes effecting this industry.

The business world evolves by the day... The challenges we faced 6 months ago just aren't as big a problem anymore and new and bigger challenges have taken their place.

If you're like most of the Coaches, Trainers and Consultants that I've spoken to so far you've probably got some big plans for the year ahead! And as with anything worth achieving there are bound to be some challenges that you come across along the way!

Just to make sure you're not in for a shock, I've identified *Three Big Threats* that you need to look out for in the new economy;

1. The cost of bringing in new clients

The first big threat to your business is the rising cost of bringing in new clients.

Like it or not, marketing and client attraction is becoming more and more expensive.

It doesn't seem that long ago that 'client attraction' was as simple as picking up the phone and making a few cold calls. It was almost easy compared to today.

Nowadays, you have to work a hell of a lot harder than you used to, to get the potential clients attention let alone make the sale!

Meaning more hours spent on the phone or at networking events.

More money invested in direct mail or online marketing. And more energy invested in getting in front of the right people!

All that effort and STILL not always getting the results you need to take your business to the next level can be frustrating!

This cost of marketing was bound to increase over the years simply because of inflation. But there are other factors influencing this trend too. Including a saturated market.

In the past, when marketing to attract clients you were only competing against yourself. General marketing always got some response and it was simply a battle against yourself to see if you can improve the results you're getting. But in today's economy you're not only competing against yourself, you're competing against the thousands of other businesses battling for the attention of your potential client.

When I first entered this industry getting the attention of a potential client was relatively easy. You'd make the odd cold call or attend the odd networking event with very little competition.

Nowadays, the typical client is greeted first thing in the morning by dozens of letters and postcards flooding through their letter boxes demanding their attention for various products and services. They open their morning paper and amongst the articles you'll see print ad after print ad again and again, demanding their attention. They'll switch on their radios on the way to work and between the clips of their favourite songs they'll have various companies battling for their attention via radio ads. During the drive to work they drive past billboards and posters advertising the latest films and events. On arriving in the office their email box will be full of businesses offering their services and promotions via email. During there working day they'll receive cold call after cold call. On arriving home, in the evening their favourite television show will be broken up with commercial breaks. Not to mention social media, YouTube and all the other marketing media that seem to be born every minute. The list really is endless. And you've no doubt experienced this from the other side. As the buyer rather than the seller. The competition for the attention of your prospects is fierce and is showing no signs of slowing down.

'Working hard' simply won't be enough for you to succeed in the years ahead. I can show you hundreds of Coaches, Trainers and Consultants who don't have as many clients as they would like and they are all some of the hardest workers you'll ever see. In today's market you need to be working hard in the right areas!

Even the more established Coaches, Trainers and Consultants have had to come to terms with the fact that things just aren't as easy as they used to be. The 'old school' will not survive in the economy.

2. Spending Reluctance

The 2nd big threat to your business profits is your potential clients and their reluctance to spend. You see, your potential clients are more careful with their money than they used to be. Meaning that even when you do get to speak to the right people, you face another uphill task actually convincing them to spend their money with you.

If you've ever met with a prospect and they seem really interested in your services, they have a clear need for what you do and you nail your sales presentation. But they still don't buy! You're witnessing spending reluctance first hand.

It's something I myself have had to battle against on many occasions and it can be extremely hard to deal with.

The first few times it happened, I left the sales meeting almost in disbelief.

I couldn't understand how someone could have a problem, I provide them with a solution that they like, and they still don't buy—it just didn't make sense to me—and it still doesn't at a level.

Some of my closest clients have shared similar frustrations with me over the years. I've lost count at the amount of times a client has called me in utter frustration that the 'sure thing' they thought they had in the bag, u-turned on a big deal and left them scratching their heads wondering where they went wrong.

Like it or not, it is something we have to come to terms with. The spending reluctance is a sociality shift that as far as I can see has affected the majority of industries in the majority of countries. The banks are more careful about who they lend money to, interest rates are higher, the business world is changing so quickly, people are desperate to hold onto their cash for as long as possible. Not to mention the effect the recession had on the way we think and behave when it comes to spending.

3. Price Pressure

The third big threat to your business profits is a little something I like to call 'Price Pressure'.

With more Coaches, Trainers and Consultants entering the industry. The truth is, no matter how you look at it, the list of competing leaders in your market is growing at a rapid pace and it doesn't look like it's going to be slowing down anytime soon.

Because of this, you can feel like you're being forced to lower your prices or keep your prices low, in order to win the business.

The power has shifted into the hands of the buyer. If they know they can get the same service you offer for cheaper down the road there is very little to convince them to buy from you.

The worst thing about these three big threats is that they almost work in sync with one another. You're not up against one of them at a time, you're constantly up against all of them. And it's can be extremely challenging at times.

Now unless you do something about it, these three threats combined will slowly drain your profits, stunt your business growth and limit the amount of cash you're able to take out of your business every month.

I have spoken to more than a few Coaches, Trainers and Consultants recently who are very seriously considering packing it all in and doing something else altogether.

But enough of the doom and gloom, because there is good news —there's always good news!

How to Protect Yourself Against These Threats

Although you can't prevent these threats per se. You can protect yourselves against them. They'll always be there. But you're in control of whether or not they have a negative impact on the future of your business.

The solution is to become exceptionally good at marketing.

If I gave you a magic wand and you had the power to attract all the clients you wanted and when you wanted. Wouldn't that remove all of your financial worries and business problems forever?

Your ability to attract clients is very important. It's the life and soul of your business and without it you have nothing. But when you get your marketing right so you can attract clients at will. You become immune to any of the threats that being in business can throw at you and success becomes a choice!

This book is your *magic wand.* And in it you'll find **everything you need to master the art of attracting clients to you as a Coach, Trainer or Consultant.**

Here's what we've covered during this chapter...

1. The real cost of bringing in new business

2. Why your potential clients are reluctant to spend

3. The danger of 'price pressure'

4. How to protect yourself against the three biggest business threats

Chapter 2
Your Attitude And Beliefs

Research has shown that this is the number one reason why some Coaches; Trainers and Consultants have so much success - even when things are tough, and all the experts are predicting doom and gloom, is their beliefs and mind-set.

Whilst others in the market are focussing on the negatives and blaming the government, the recession and the tight fisted banks for their struggles. The successful Coach, Trainer or Consultant steps up, takes responsibility for their own situation and asks themselves more empowering questions.

Questions such as:

- ✓ Over the next 90 days, what three things can we do to increase sales?
- ✓ Who are the 100 top potential clients we should speak to?
- ✓ What seven things am I grateful for right now in my life?

Initially when I first sat down to write this book I wanted it purely to be about marketing and what you can do to attract clients.

Don't worry, that will come. But in order for any of what I share with you in later chapters to work it's important that I first make you aware of your beliefs and your mind-set.

The way you think dictates the way you act, the way you act dictates the actions you take, and the actions you take dictate your results.

Without the right attitude you won't take the appropriate action and therefore won't get the results you're looking for.

Attitudes drive behaviour. Your results are the result of your mental attitude. When you choose your attitude, you consciously (or unconsciously) send out that message and it's loud and clear for people to see.

Almost always, you have a choice as to what attitude to adopt. There is nothing in any normal work situation that dictates you must react one way or another. If you feel angry about something that happens, that's how you choose to feel. Nothing in the event itself makes it absolutely necessary for you to feel that way, it's your choice. And since you do have a choice, most of the time you'll be better off if you choose to react in a positive, rather than a negative way.

People spend a lifetime searching for happiness; looking for peace. They chase idle dreams, addictions, religions and even other people, hoping to fill the emptiness that plagues them. The irony is the only place they ever needed to search was within.

The Power of Positive Attitude

It's not what happens to you that counts; it's how you react to what happens to you, especially when you experience unexpected problems of any kind. Learn and master powerful mind strategies you can use to keep yourself thinking and acting positively and creatively.

Positive attitude means longer life

If you want to live a longer healthier life, then you need to develop and maintain a positive attitude. It's now a fact, thanks to a study from two American Universities.

Researchers followed and studied 1500 people for seven years. All 1500 were in good health when the study started. They studied how they aged, by measuring such things as weight loss, walking speed, and exhaustion.

What exactly did they discover? They found that people who maintained a positive attitude were significantly less likely to show signs of aging were less likely to become frail and were more likely to be stronger and healthier than those who had a negative attitude. If you have a doom and gloom attitude you're actually killing yourself, and at the very least, your negative attitude is just making you weaker.

So if you want a successful Coaching, Training and Consultancy business, make a decision today to be happy and successful. It's your choice.

Resolve

Imagine this...

It's your wedding day and instead of your partner saying "I DO!" They say, "I'll *try*".

Not the kind of commitment you'd expect to see from your partner on your wedding day is it?

The same applies to your business! Coaches, Trainers and Consultants think, talk and do in terms of '*trying*' to generate leads and '*trying*' to grow their business.

Being committed to trying isn't good enough. **You need to be committed to DOING.**

Successful Coaches, Trainers and Consultants owners don't just 'TRY' to be successful, they are *100% committed to DOING!* And so, everyday they make decisions others are not willing to make in order to achieve their goal and they continue to make decisions that others are not willing to make in order to stay successful.

Like it or not, the business environment we now operate in can be harsh, cutthroat and competitive.

And it seems to be becoming more and more competitive by the day.

And I'm not just talking about competing businesses;

- ⮑ Today, you're competing against the economy.

- ⮑ You're competing against your personal challenges.

- ⮑ You're competing against your potential clients and their reluctance to spend any money.

- ⮑ It's a never-ending list and it's growing by the day.

So if you think, talk and do in terms of *'trying'*. When the proverbial hits the fan, as it will at more than one point in your business life, you're not going to have the resolve to get through it.

If you read the biography of any successful person in any industry, whether they're successful in the business world, sports world, music industry, whichever, almost without exception, there's a point in their life or career when they are pretty much at rock bottom! They have businesses that have been bankrupt or close to bankruptcy.

They've had career threatening injuries or they're dropped from the team. They get dropped from their record label or their songs don't sell. Whatever it may be, they, as does everyone else on this planet, have some very big obstacles to overcome in order to achieve what it is they set out to achieve.

Do you think that if they had just been 'TRYING' to be successful they would have had the strength to pick themselves up and turn things around?

Or course not!

Their commitment and resolve kept them going while all of the 'Try-ers' gave up and fell by the way side.

And it's the same for you...

**Don't just 'TRY'. Be 100% committed and be willing to
do the things that others are not willing to do and
make the decisions that others are not willing to make.**

Here's what we've covered during this chapter...

1. The power of positive attitude

2. The importance of real resolve and commitment

Chapter 3
Not Knowing Where Your Business Is Going

"People with goals succeed because they know where they are going. It's as simple as that."
Earl Nightingale

For most of the Coaches, Trainers and Consultants I speak to. *'Goal Setting'* is old hat. It's something they know, it's something they teach and it's something they heavily endorse to their clients. But as human beings we don't always practice what we preach.

Whist writing this book, I've been reminded of many things that I know I should be doing, many strategies and techniques that I know work. But for whatever reason I'm not using them as effectively as I should in my own business.

I've found 'goal setting' to be one of the many forgotten strategies with the Coaches, Trainers and Consultants I come across.

One of the biggest reasons most independent Coaching, Training and Consultancy businesses fail is:

➲ They don't know where they're going and if you don't know where you're going how will you know when you get there?

Let me explain.

Nearly every audio program, video program, book and seminar on the subject of personal development and business success covers the idea of goal setting.

And yet, despite all the information available about this subject, I've found over the years that, most Coaches, Trainers and Consultants have not set goals for their business.

For those who have written their goals on paper, many of them haven't kept up to date with the actions or measured them against good records as to where they are against their goals.

It's often been said that successful people set goals.

I've been very fortunate, over the years, to have interviewed many successful Coaches, Trainers and Consultants. The one thing that seems to be the common theme amongst them is that they each have a well-defined goal so they know exactly where they're going.

A story for you...

There is an alleged story from 1954. A group of students who were graduating from Harvard University were asked a series of questions. One of these questions was: *"Do you have a well-defined goal that's written down?"*

87% said that they did NOT have goals, 10% said that they had goals but that those goals weren't written down, and only 3% said that they had WRITTEN goals.

Some 20 years later these same respondents were interviewed and asked a variety of questions about their lives. The 3%, who had written their goals down all those years before, were now worth more when put together, than the other 97%.

Now you and I know that money is only one measure of success, and that every single person can have his or her own definition of success. What was also interesting about this study was that the 3% who had well-defined goals were happier and more content than the entire 97%.

It must make you think that there really is something about goal setting that makes a major difference to us as Coaches,

Trainers and Consultants and therefore to our individual success.

In all the years I've been working with Coaches, Trainers and Consultants, I have never ever met a successful business owner who *didn't have a well-defined goal,* and who didn't know exactly what the business would look; sound and feel like when it was finished.

Why People Don't Set Goals

So before we look at how to set our goals, let's look at the reasons why people don't set them, and why, if they do, some people don't keep them up to date.

Over the years I've asked thousands of Coaches, Trainers and Consultants why they don't set goals and below is a sample of the answers.

Perhaps if you haven't yet set goals, or if you have but struggled to keep up to date with them, this might help you identify some of the reasons why!

- They don't know how to do it.
- They fear failure.
- They fear success, perhaps believing that success brings more problems, that their friends will be jealous and stop liking them.
- They're too impatient, - but as you and I know success comes one step at a time.
- They think their major goals are unattainable.
- Fear of rejection.
- They don't make time to do it.
- They have self-limiting beliefs.

- They think that goal setting isn't important.
- They have no ambition.

So knowing that goal setting is important, here are some areas for you to consider setting goals for:

- Career
- Skill improvement
- Time usage
- Fitness
- Health
- Personal relationships
- Leisure
- Sports
- Travel
- Commercial goals
- Financial success
- Learning to speak in public
- Increasing vocabulary
- Negotiation or selling skills
- Management skills
- Body language
- Creativity

Goal setting is for anything and everything you want to achieve.

It's essential that your personal goals are in alignment with your commercial goals.

The most common goal setting areas are what I call the 3 F"s:

1. Fitness
2. Finance/business
3. Family

It has been found that having goals in these three areas brings balance and fulfilment to your life.

The Reticular Activation System

The marvellous thing about setting goals, having a direction, and knowing what we want, is that we engage a part of our brain called the Reticular Activation System

I'm sure you'll have had the following happen to you:

You've decided to buy something, and then suddenly you see that same item everywhere. Perhaps the commonest occurrence of this is when you're about to take delivery of a new car. Suddenly you see that same car everywhere, the same model, even the same colour!

Why?

Simply because you've opened your mind to that information.

Perhaps you've booked a holiday and then start to see information about that place that you've never noticed before.

Once we focus on something, then we notice more about that subject or object. That's what happens when we set goals. We start to hear and see things that will help us to achieve them. Those things were there before; we just didn't know that we needed them because we hadn't set our goals and told ourselves that we were interested in that information.

So let's look at some of the best ways to set goals:

1. Goals must be written down

Why?

Simply because once they're written down you can audit them. You can read them on a regular basis; you can check that you're on track to their accomplishment. If they're not written down, they're just dreams, not goals!

2. When you write your goals, make certain that they're written in positive language, without linguistic negatives and in the present tense.

Positive Language

If you write goals in negative language or use linguistic negatives it's extremely hard for your mind to form a picture of the outcome you want.

Can you form a picture for the word 'not', meaning not doing something? It's difficult to do. It's far better to create a picture of what you want and use the power of language to provide a clear picture.

If you have a goal to give up something, then instead of saying: *"I will not smoke,"* which can only reinforce the habit, re word *it, to a reward based goal like; "I would like to have a healthy body"* or *"my partner enjoys holding me as I smell so much better."*

Write goals in the present tense, rather than the future tense

If you set a goal that says, *"I will be..."* or *"I will have..."*

The words – *"will be"* or *"will have"*, indicate something in the future, not something that will ever come to pass. So every time you read the goal it will always be positioned in the future. It's far better to say, *"The date is..."* and state a future date while using the terms *"I have"* or *"I am"* or *"I do."*

This method sets up internal pressure to perform.

So to recap:

- ✓ Positive language
- ✓ No linguistic negatives.
- ✓ Present tense

Which goals to go for?

Here is a very simple process, which you can use immediately:

Decide on a time frame that you want to work with; that could be one year, five years, ten years, or even a lifetime – you decide.

Then write a question at the top of a clean page which asks: *"What do I want to have, be and do in this time frame?"*

Then brainstorm, or brain-dump every idea you have, including places you want to go, achievements, profits, as well as personal, commercial, social or anything and everything you can think of.

3. Prioritizing your goals

Now you need to prioritize that list, and the way to do it varies, depending upon the length of the list.

If the list is short, about six or seven items, then you can easily prioritize it using numbers. If the list is long, start by simply categorizing which of the three areas each one falls into A, B or C.

- A. Goals you definitely want to achieve.
- B. You would like to achieve
- C. Well maybe one day you'll get round to them.

Write down what it is that you want, not what is expected of you. Then take the "A" list and prioritize that with numbers.

Ok, so let's take just your top goal and look how that should be written down. Remember that a goal is only a stake in the ground. It gives you direction, and because it's your goal you can change it at any time. Be bold, there's not much fun in achieving inconsequential goals.

Here are the steps to write out your goals, write the goal down using this formula, and make sure your goals are:

- ✓ Precise
- ✓ Exciting
- ✓ Truthful
- ✓ Effective action
- ✓ Recordable/measurable
- ✓ Affirmation (letter to the future)

The Science of Goal Setting

1. Precise - The goal must be precise otherwise it's difficult to take aim.

There's little point saying we want to be rich without knowing precisely what rich means. Obviously, rich has different meanings for different people.

So ensure that your goal has all the numbers, dates and details included, so that you know precisely what you're aiming for.

2. Exciting - The goal must be exciting.

Why? Because, if the goal doesn't move you in some way, you're unlikely to stay on track. However, if it does excite you, it's far more likely that you'll continue to take action until the goal is achieved. I'll give some more detail on this part further on.

3. Truthful - The goal must be truthful.

By this I mean that you must really believe that you can achieve it. As you and I know, if we don't believe that we can do something, that belief is going to stop us taking action.

So, a self-question about your belief in yourself to achieve this goal will be necessary.

4. Effective Action - The goal should involve you in Effective Action.

Yes, you may well need to involve other people in helping you achieve your goal, but there must be personal commitment to action; action that will take you to your goal; not just any old action, but effective action.

Action that is clearly focused on you achieving the goal, keeping you on track, ensuring your success.

5. Recordable - The goal must be recordable, and recordable in two specific ways.

a) You must be able to measure or record that you have achieved the goal of course,

b) You must be able to measure your progress along the way.

Example

Imagine for a moment that you'd set a goal to go on holiday to a certain country on a certain date. You would need to know how much that trip would cost and how much, if you had to save for it, you would need to save each month or each year. That way you could measure your progress towards the goal by the monthly saving and your eventual achievement of the goal of going to the country in question.

Once you've written your goal in this way you'll know that it is precise and exciting, you believe that YOU can achieve it and that you'll need to take effective action that you can measure.

With good records you'll achieve the goal, because you'll know where you are at any time, regarding the actions and results you're achieving.

6. Affirmation/Letter to the future - The final part of the goal setting process is to write an affirmation/letter to the future.

This is simply a paragraph that affirms to yourself that you will take the actions you've decided to take, that you will achieve the goal, and that the actions and result are in alignment, with your values and beliefs.

Write a letter to your Coach as if it is the date you have achieved your goal. Write your goal and letter to the future in the present tense. *"I am"* rather than *"I will"*. They must include the date to be specific and they must be written in positive. Remember think about what you want. Use words like *"I love doing"* and *"I am"*.

Taking Action

> *"It's not knowing what to do, it's doing what you know."*
> Tony Robbins

So you've set your well-defined goals and you know exactly what your business will look like in one to five years from now.

If you believe that's it, I have some news for you. Setting the goal is only the first step. ***Now you must take ACTION***. Once you know where your business is going, you can now look at, and decide on the action steps that you'll need to take to achieve your goals. *Deciding what you're going to do and when, will bring results.*

Here's what we've covered during this chapter...

1. Why people don't set goals
2. The reticular activation system
3. The science of goal setting

Chapter 4
The 7 Golden Rules Of Marketing

I'm quite a laid back individual. It takes a lot to wind me up to the point of no return. And the older I get and the wiser I become, fewer things tend to get my back up. But there are still a few things that really piss me off!

It happens every now and then - the frustration gets too much and I feel like I want to explode! It doesn't happen quite as often as it used to, but when it does you can be sure someone's going to get a piece of my mind at the very least.

And this morning, in an email from a potential client, it happened! Here's the question you can ask me to get my blood boiling:

"What's the ONE THING I can do to take Coaching, Training or Consultancy Business to the next level"

They weren't the exact words used. But the sentiment is still the same. The idea that to grow an extraordinary successful business in today's economy could come down to doing just ONE thing is criminal! Having that belief is damaging and in my view is **one of the biggest reasons** that so many Coaches, Trainers and Consultants never reach their full potential!

Thinking that you can go out there and just dabble at this. Just do one or two things and suddenly things will start happening for you is far from the reality.

To take your business to the next level takes relentless commitment.

Real resolve as I mentioned earlier!

If it came down to doing just one thing, it would be too easy, - everyone would be doing it!

But breaking through the barriers and taking your business to the next level is NOT easy! Not by a long stretch! The ONE THING is EVERYTHING!

Saying that, there are a set of **golden rules** you can follow to ensure you're always on the right path. These rules form the backbone of everything I teach and have the potential to transform the way you currently do things in your business'

The Dirty 'M' word

There's a dirty 'M' word that no- one likes to say...

Coaches, Trainers and Consultants will go out of their way to avoid it, not realizing the negative impact it's having on their business profits—And that word is '*marketing*'— Filthy!

I've lost count of the number of Coaches, Trainers or Consultants I meet who say they don't like marketing. Or who will spend their time doing everything BUT marketing because they don't know or don't care how important it really is.

The only difference between a successful Coach, Trainer or Consultant and those who struggle is *effective marketing activity.*

And when I say 'effective,' I mean profitable. As in marketing activity that adds profits to your business and NOT just activity that wastes time and money.

And when it comes to effective marketing there's nothing new.

What works and what doesn't work has been known for some time.

No matter what anyone tells you, there's no 'new' way of marketing and attracting clients because it all comes down to basic human psychology.

The fundamentals ALWAYS stay the same. That's why you call them fundamentals.

It doesn't matter whether you're using the telephone to attract clients or social media, the basic rules always apply.

The only thing that changes is the media you use.

The problem is, most Coaches, Trainers and Consultants in the market get the fundamentals wrong... So it doesn't matter what media they use, they always get the same disappointing results and can't seem to grow their business quickly enough.

And so despite working long hard hours they end up losing clients just as quickly as they can bring them in. And either end up standing still or with a feast and famine, yo-yo income.

If you've ever experienced anything remotely similar it's because you're breaking the rules and you're getting the fundamentals wrong.

Golden Rule Number 1: Brand Advertising VS Direct Response

There are two styles of marketing.

And if you're finding your marketing isn't getting a response it might be because you're engaging in one rather than the other.

You see, most Coaches, Trainers and Consultants in the market engage in what's commonly known as '*Brand Advertising.*'

Brand Advertising is all about getting you, your brand, your company colours and your logo out there for the world to see in the hope that it's somehow going to attract the right attention and cause people to give you their business at will.

The problem with that is...

Most of the time, people aren't actually looking for you or your services at all.

No, they're looking for a 'headache cure' rather than 'advil'.

So if you go around marketing your brand of aspirin with all its fancy colours and logos more often than not it gets ignored!

All your prospects really care about is themselves and their problems.

That's why, one of the biggest mistakes you can make as a Coach, Trainer or Consultant is having your marketing messages plastered with YOUR logo and YOUR company details and YOUR 'amazing' qualities, it's a waste of time, paper and ink.

The only marketing you should be doing is *'direct response'* marketing; that is, **every single marketing activity you engage in should be for one reason and one reason only**;

➲   To get a **direct response** from the potential client

Meaning they will;

✓   Pick up the phone and call you...

✓   They'll come into your office...

✓   They fill out a form on a website...

✓   Anything that requires a response...

In other words, you get **direct, clear and measurable response.**

And that's the other thing about 'Brand Advertising'. It's all but *impossible to measure.* A million people could see your company name and logo but you'd have no way of knowing whether or not any one of them will buy from you off the back of it!

Think about your typical television ad for instance, and I'm not talking about infomercials where there is often a very clear and precise call to action making it 'Direct Response Marketing'. I'm talking about the typical television ad that you might see from the likes of Coca Cola around Christmas time.

This is a prime example of 'Brand Advertising'. Firstly, it often costs millions to do! Something that most small business in any industry can't afford and sure, you'll get to see their logo and their company name.

But does this equal more sales?

I suspect not and even if sales did happen to go up during the period the ad was being displayed. There's no way of knowing whether people were buying directly off the back off the ad!

And that's not to say that branding doesn't have a place— Because it does—Especially for the bigger corporate companies with a very wide target audience like Coca Cola.

But for you as a Coach, Trainer or Consultant it's not something you should be thinking about until AFTER the sale is made and you have the customer.

Brand Advertising does not equal leads. Direct Response marketing does!

Golden Rule Number 2: Your Market Is NOT Different

"But... My market is different."

That short statement above is probably the one I hear most often from the Coaches, Trainers and Consultants I come across.

Somehow, somewhere along the line, they've come to the misconception that their business is different.

And even though the marketing and client attraction strategies I teach have repeatedly worked for so many businesses like theirs, in various parts of the world, in various economic climates they believe it won't work for them because '*Their market is different*'.

It's complete and total nonsense, and actually makes no sense if you think about it!

As long as you're selling to people with a brain... And I mean that in the literal sense here.

Your market IS exactly the same!

That is as long as you're selling to human beings, regardless of children or adults; males or females; fat or thin; a stay at home parent; or a busy C level executive they have the same core factors of influence and the same emotional pulls.

No matter who it is that you target, it's a matter of changing the style not the substance

In fact, some of the most successful marketing campaigns EVER to work for Coaches, Trainers and Consultants, have been heavily influenced by campaigns used in other industries. The style changed and adapted to fit, but the substance stays the same.

I once had a client who, when he first started working with me thought his market was too sophisticated for my 'kind' of marketing. He specialised in working with solicitors, and people in the legal sector and had somehow got it into his head that his audience were a different breed of human. Too smart and too advanced to be influenced by the same principles that have influenced humans since the beginning of time. He wasn't alone in his beliefs. I hear it all the time even still today.

But it's worth remembering no matter who you target. The big important CEO that purchased that luxury yacht, is the same person who goes to his local shop and buys milk and the morning paper, he's the same person who goes to his local pub and orders a pint across the bar, he's the same person that ordered jewellery for his wife online, he's the same person who takes his car into the garage for repair, he's the same person that likes beans on toast as his lunchtime meal, he's the same person that supports his local sports team. Without exception we are all influenced by the same basic principles and it's just a matter of *putting the right message in front of the right market,* using the *right media at the right time*. The substance always stays the same.

Golden Rule Number 3: The Two Profitable Habits

Traditionally, human beings are creatures of habits, we pick up new ones and work at losing old ones. We have good ones and we have bad ones. We're all the same in that sense. The difference lies in which habits we adopt. You see, in any walk of life it's the repeated behaviours that get you the overall outcome. For example, an Olympian has gotten into the habit of training regularly and eating the right foods. Whereas someone who is overweight, has got into the habit of being lazy, not exercising and eating foods that are bad for them. Someone who has lots of money in the bank has gotten into the habit of saving more than they spend, whereas someone with debt has got into the habit of spending more than they save. Any results in any given situation is the outcome of repeating the same behaviours over and over again. Almost to the point that we do them without even giving them too much thought.

One thing I've noticed in the all successful Coaches, Trainers and Consultants I've come across, there are **two good habits** that they have in common. They've all fallen into the habit of both *education* and *implementation*. And it makes sense when you think about it because you can't really be successful in anything without BOTH of these habits forming the very core of everything you do.

Take education for example...

Let's say you're struggling to attract all the clients you need. And you've tried all that you know to turn things around but nothing is quite having the desired effect.

Perhaps you've never previously been taught how to attract clients. Or perhaps what you have been taught is out-dated and doesn't work as well as it used to.

What's the solution?

You pick up some books, hit the Internet, maybe even learn from another professional in your field who has proven results, and you educate yourself of what's working!

And because the world of marketing and client attraction is ever changing, the education doesn't stop there. It's a continuous process that NEVER stops.

EVER!

And that's part of the problem for the majority of Coaches, Trainers and Consultants who don't have all the clients they need.

They perhaps learn one method for attracting clients and then they rely on it for years and years as it slowly becomes more and more out-dated and eventually stops working completely...

The education never stops! It needs to become a repeated behaviour just like going to the gym regularly is for Olympians and just like you brush your teeth at the end of the day. Education is a repeated behaviour for the successful Coaches, Trainers and Consultants.

If you think about it, the more successful professionals in this industry know more about marketing and client attraction than most.

Yet learning newer and more effective techniques forms a very, very big part of what they do...And that's partly why they're so successful.

But only partly, because education will only get you so far.

You need **implementation** too. Because learning all that stuff counts for sweet FA if you *do nothing* with it.

You can have all the knowledge and 'know how' in the world.... You need *to do something with that knowledge* if you ever want to get results.

One of the most frustrating things I hear when I'm speaking to Coaches, Trainers and Consultants about growing their business is:

"But I know that already..."

The important thing when it comes to growing your business isn't whether you know it or not, it's whether you actually take action on what it is that you know.

I'm sure in this book I'm going to talk about things you've heard before. but just because you've heard something before it does not give you permission to discount it as unimportant.

Successful Coaches, Trainers and Consultants are serial implementers. They just get stuff done and they get stuff done quickly.

You won't see them faffing around waiting for their fancy website to be finished.

They don't spend weeks on end trying to find the perfect paper for a direct mail piece.

Or the right subject line for an email...

All of which are genuine real life examples of the excuses I hear for not doing something. They get stuff done!

They implement what they know!

But implementation on it's own can be dangerous. Because without the education to go with it, all you end up doing is implementing the wrong things in the wrong places.

Something that is all too familiar in this industry...

So you see, *'Education'* and *'Implementation'* go very much hand in hand and are two of the habits I recommend you adopt going forward.

Education and Implementation form the core of everything I do with the clients I work with. It's what allows them to drive their business forward at a rate their competitors can only be envious of.

Golden Rule Number 4: The Number 'One' Is The Worst Number In Your Business

Recently, one of my clients contacted me in some distress.

You see he had just lost his biggest client... And with it, a VERY large chunk of his projected profits for the year...Ouch!

Losing a client like that can be a big hit!

And one that I've seen even some of the more established Coaches, Trainers and Consultants struggle to get up from.

But as always, there is a very important lesson to learn here, it's a lesson I had to re-learn for myself more than once, quite recently in fact!

But sometimes business life throws these things up again and again, and you have to re-learn it!

The thing is, no matter how good you are at what you do you will lose clients from time to time and it's outside of your control, so there's often not much you can do about it.

The only solution is to protect yourself, so when it does happen, it's not such a big hit...

The worst number in your business is **ONE!** That's *one* key member of staff, *one* route to market, or in this case *one* key client.

Any time you see the number one in your business, you are at risk!

I would consider myself an optimistic person, but despite that, in business, you have to be wary of what might happen. There are always going to be risks in business, they're unavoidable. But the smart Coaches, Trainers and Consultants protect themselves against them.

Golden Rule Number 5: The Only Three Ways To Grow Your Business

There are three and *only three* ways to grow your business. Most Coaches, Trainers and Consultants tend to only focus on one (if any at all!).

1. *Getting* more clients

2. *Increase the transaction frequency* (how often they spend money)

3. *Increase how much they spend* each time they buy (your prices)

Getting more clients

When it comes to increasing profits and growing a business, getting more customers and clients tends to be the only area the typical Coach, Trainer or Consultant focuses on. Simply put, they know more clients equal more money. And so all their time and effort tends to be put into this area. This might surprise you to hear but not only is 'getting more clients' only one of three ways to grow your business. It's also usually the hardest. Even for an experienced marketer, doubling the number of clients they currently have in six months would be an almost unrealistic ask.

Increase the transaction frequency (how often they spend)

For the typical business model for Coaches, Trainers and Consultants who work on a monthly contract, this would translate to your retention rate. For example, your working relationship with a new client would typically last for 10 months with them paying you a set fee each month. If you can increase the relationship length from 10 months to 13 months you would increase the amount of money you take of each client and therefore your business revenue would increase.

Increase how much they spend each time they buy (your prices)

The third and final way to increase your business revenue is to increase the amount your client spends with you each time they spend. In other words - your prices.

Going back to the example above. If your client pays you a set fee of $1000 per month. Assuming they still stay with you for the same amount of time, increasing that set fee to $2000 per month would increase your revenue.

Let's do the math. (I'm going to use $ as the currency but this would translate to whatever local currency you use.)

Scenario 1: Example current business revenue

10 Clients

10 Months (average)

$1000 (average per month)

Business revenue = $100,000

Scenario 2: 10% Increase across the board

10 Clients + 10% = 11

10 Months + 10% = 11

$1000 + 10% = $1100

New business revenue = $133,100

Scenario 3: Maximum 30% increase

10 Clients + 30% =13

10 Months + 30% =13

1000 + 20% = $1200

New business revenue = $202,800 (more than double what we originally started with)

You can quickly see how important working on all three areas simultaneously becomes. If you're just focusing on one of these three things you're making things difficult for yourself and leaving money on the table.

Golden Rule Number 6: Testing and Measuring

Not long ago, a colleague of mine was telling me about one of his old girl friends and it reminded me of a friend of mine...

...You might even have a friend with similar qualities.

She had graduated from a business school somewhere, after studying 'marketing' for four years...

(I put the word 'Marketing' in inverted commas because you have never really studied marketing, until you get out in the big bad business world and experience the pain, and heartache of losing money first hand when you get a marketing campaign wrong and also the joy and profits when you get it right!)

Anyway... Because she had studied marketing in the cotton wool surroundings that is the lecture halls you'll find in most educational establishments, she somehow thought this made her opinion useful to me. When in reality, practically every idea, solution and opinion she had about my emails, my website, the way I conducted business—all of it—were dead wrong!

And I knew that because I'd been ignoring her advice for some time and seen the profit to prove I had made the right decision.

At first, it was amusing.

But soon, it got annoying and grated away at me like a rusty potato peeler. Until one day, I had an idea for making her opinion useful.

What I would do is, I would ask her what she thought of an email I was going to send to my list or an ad headline or a product idea I was playing with, etc. and then I would do the exact opposite!

And it worked!

I made more profits for me and the Coaches, Trainers and Consultants I worked with. (I should perhaps thank her for the non-business advice she's given me over the years because I can honestly say it's helped me immensely!)

Anyway, moral of the story?

If you know a 'marketing' graduate who hasn't yet tested their theory's in the big bad business world and not yet figured out that pretty much everything they learned in the classroom is useless, get their opinion...

...And do the opposite!

In reality there really is no place for opinions in marketing

Yes of course people will naturally form opinions based on past experience. But all opinions (including mine) count for nothing unless they've been *tried and tested* in the big bad world.

The truth is, some of the strategies I'll share with you in this book will work better for you than they will for others. And some will work better for others than they do for you. But you will never know until you test.

Taking Testing To Another Level:

There are *two levels* when it comes to testing.

1. You can test the strategies in question. For example. You could test using email, you could test direct mail, and you could test using the telephone.

2. You can test techniques within the strategies. E.g. You can test sending an email at 9:00am vs. sending an email at 11:30am and see which one gets the best response.

Testing and measuring should form a core part of what you do when marketing your business. It's the only way to get continuous improvement over time.

Golden Rule Number 7: The Investor Mind-set

"If for every £20 you gave me, I gave you £100 back. when would you stop giving me money?"

A few years ago I attended a seminar on marketing. It's something that I do quite regularly but this particular seminar stands out in my mind because at the time it led to a major breakthrough in the way I viewed marketing and subsequently led to a major breakthrough in my business and the businesses of the Coaches, Trainers and Consultants I work with.

Right at the beginning of the presentation, the presenter asked the room if anyone had a £20 note.

One volunteer at the front of the room, put his hand up and was pulled on stage.

The presenter then took the £20 pound note out of the volunteer's hand and then handed him five more £20 notes in return.

And then asked the question:

"If for every £20 you gave me, I gave you £100 back... When would you stop giving me money?"

The answer is, you wouldn't!

Because you know you're getting a return on your investment (ROI).

The day you truly grasp that marketing your business is an *investment* rather than a *cost* is the day you'll set yourself free financially.

Sure, you'll still be restricted by cash flow on occasions, but when you can run marketing campaigns for as little as a few dollars or pounds a day, there's never a reason to view it as a cost.

It's an investment.

And it's probably the best investment you'll ever make because unlike stocks and shares or property for example you are essentially in control of the return you get.

And in comparison to most traditional investments where the return can be quite small, if you see any at all, the return on investment on marketing can be hundreds of percent! (my ROI from LinkedIn PPC for example is *over 700%*)

As a Coach, Trainer or Consultant your job role also doubles up as a professional investor. You should be investing in buying customers, and providing your income and profit is *higher than the cost of investment,* your future is secure...

Here's what we've covered during this chapter...

1. The dirty 'M' word

2. Brand advertising VS direct response

3. Your market is not different

4. The two profitable habits

5. The number one is the worst number in your business

6. The only three ways to grow your business

7. Testing & Measuring

8. The investor mind-set

Chapter 5
The Coaches, Trainers and Consultants Lead Rush System

Behind every successful Coach, Trainer and Consultant is a well-oiled marketing machine. A system that continues to provide predictable and scalable results over and over again. It's a process.

A lot of Coaches, Trainers and Consultants have no real system or process and try to move too quickly, often repelling their potential client.

When describing this, many of my colleagues in the marketing world use the 'dating' analogy. Like dating, love and romance... Sales and Marketing is a seduction too.

When you do it right, it turns strangers into friends and friends into lifetime clients.

So whether you're trying to get a date in time for Valentine's day, or you're trying to add profits to your business, mastering these next seven principles of seduction will work in your favour.

7 Principles of Seduction

1. Market: Know your 'type'

In the dating world, before you can hope to attract your ideal. You've got to know who your ideal partner is. The way you do things and the way you operate means you're going to be most attracted to a certain demographic of people. By the same token, a certain demographic of people are going to be attracted to you and the way you do things. Your business should be no different. The more information you know about your 'type', the easier it will be to seduce them.

2. Message: Your opening line

In the dating world initiating the conversation is half the battle. The key is to find something that your ideal partner is interested in and hone in on it. Marketing your business is no different. Rather than talking about you, you need a message that talks directly to the wants and desires of your ideal client.

3. Media: How to reach your 'type'

The media you use to meet your ideal partner is very important. For example, let's say your 'type' is single women aged between 35-45. You're probably not going to find many of them in the male locker room at your gym. Get the media wrong and you end up attracting the wrong sort of people and could potentially get yourself into all sorts of uncompromising positions.

4. Irresistible Offer: Get their interest

If you're in your local singles bar, this could be as simple as offering to buy your target a drink. If they say *"no"* to the drink then you move onto the next target. If they say *"Yes"* this is a good indication that they're interested in your message and want to continue the conversation. In the business world rather than a drink you could consider offering them free information of some sort that will help them overcome the problem they're facing.

5. Lead Capture: Get their details

Once you've got their interest, you need some way of capturing the lead. In the dating world this could be as simple as taking down their phone number so you can follow up on that interest with a call. The business world is no different and follows the exact same principle.

6. Short Term Follow Up: Nurturing the relationship

In step 4 and 5 you've got your targets' attention and they agreed to further communication from you. Step 6 is all about nurturing that relationship with the hope of 'closing the deal'

7. Long Tem Follow Up: Lead Maintenance

The final step follows a similar process to previous (Short Term Follow Up: Nurturing The Relationship). It's all about closing the deal. Ideally, the sale is made in step six but the reality is, some of your prospects will take more convincing before you 'can close the deal'. It's important to continuously reinforce the incentive. Over time any incentive wears out, just like your date may tire of the finest restaurant, the potential client may tire from your approach too.

But it doesn't stop there because this isn't about getting a string of one night stands or one off sales, this is about maximizing profits and therefore you need to be building long term lasting relationships with your clients over time. So they buy and buy again.

Let's take a more detailed look at each of these seven steps:

1. Market: Know Your 'Type'

When starting out as a Coach, Trainer or Consultant, the first question that we often ask ourselves is what service are we going to sell and how are we going to sell it?

Although they are two important questions, the first question we *should* be asking ourselves is not *"what"* but *"who"*.

The *"who are we going to sell to?"* question is often a secondary one and it's one that we often only give a half- hearted answer to, if we bother answering it at all.

But knowing 'who' you sell to is *very important* because it's probably the biggest deciding factor in the potential of your business, it's something that requires your constant attention and it's something you need to be looking at continuously.

You see, 'who' you sell to needs to be *directly in line* with what it is you want to achieve for four reasons;

1. It determines the *upper limits* on your potential wealth
2. It determines the *speed of growth* in your business
3. It determines how *easy or difficult* it is to grow your business
4. It determines your *overall message* marketing strategy

Take these two businesses for example:

You could be a Business Coach who works with small to medium sized business owners based in the small British town of Northampton.

Or...

You could be a Business Coach who works with big blue chip organisations across the world.

Both businesses essentially offer the same service but their source of clients will be very different, which means the upper limits on their business growth would be different, the potential speed at which they can grow will be different, the ease of growth will be different and so would their overall marketing strategy.

Who you sell to forms the foundation for everything else you do in your business. Get the foundations wrong and everything else you do can fall to pieces very quickly.

This in my view is one of the biggest reasons so many Coaches, Trainers and Consultants don't have as many clients as they would like and struggle to take their business to the level they want it to be. They're getting the 'who?' wrong

Your Source Of Clients

One thing that a lot of Coaches, Trainers and Consultants neglect to put much thought into is their source of clients.

Which is a shame, because it's an area that requires just as much thought as any other area when it comes to your business growth, if not more!

Your source of clients very directly impacts the upper limits in your potential wealth.

Just to make sure we're on the same page here, when I say *'source of clients'* I'm referring to the size and demographics of your target audience.

The size of your target audience and the number of people you can reach is very important and should probably be the first thing you look at when deciding on how you're going to market your business.

One of my oldest clients used to only target business owners in his local town. Nothing wrong with that of course, and assuming you're good at what you do you can make a very good living indeed doing that, but at the same time, you have to realise that there is a limit.

Your potential wealth is limited to the size of your target audience. No matter how good you are at sales, marketing and client attraction there is always going to be only a certain number of people who can buy what you sell.

For example, if there are only a total of two hundred or so potential clients in your 'business universe', you have a different upper limit compared to if there were two thousand potential clients that you could work with!

There is no right or wrong answer to who your source of potential clients should be. But be very aware that whatever decision you make will have a direct impact on the upper limits of your wealth and your business as a Coach, Trainer or Consultant.

So *"Who And What Are Your Dream Clients?"*

This is a question only you can answer. There are no rules here, your 'Dream 100' may have different characteristics to mine or anyone else's. This is for you to choose and it's your decision only, but this is certainly a decision that will be more profitable than any others.

Here are some things to consider when choosing your Dream 100 clients:

Geography

Where are your ideal clients based?

You may find that your ideal clients tend to be located in a specific location. For example: if you target globally, you might find that your ideal clients tend to reside in one particular country or one particular continent. If you target locally, you may find that your ideal clients tend to be located in a particular area of town.

Number of employees/company size

How many people does your ideal client employ?

Another thing you may want to consider when choosing your 'Dream 100' is the size of the company and organizational structure. Again, there is no right or wrong answer here, but it's important you find the answer that is right for you.

It's also important that you know WHO within that organization has the power to make the decision to buy from you. Targeting the wrong people within an organization can waste both your time and money.

Company Turnover

How much revenue does your ideal client generate per year?

Usually, the higher the revenue the better. More revenue usually means that the company has more to spend on outside services such as yours. Smaller revenues means tighter budgets and it being less likely that they are able to afford you. Even if they can afford you, when they have to make cuts, you'll be one of the first to go!

But *What If I Don't Know?*

If you're fairly new in business or you have no idea who your ideal clients are, then there are two things you can do;

Firstly, you can look back at your past clients, look at the ones who were worth more to you; look at the ones who stayed with you longer; look at the ones who paid you the most money and look for similar characteristics between them, their business size, location, organizational culture etc. The more similarities you can find, the better!

This will give you a rough guide to the type of business you should be targeting with your 'Dream 100' campaigns.

And secondly, if you're starting from scratch and have no past clients make an educated guess, taking into consideration the areas we looked at earlier. Modify your answer as you learn more about your market. As a starting point, it's usually the bigger businesses who fit the criteria.

The thing with smaller organizations is that cash flow is often an issue and when cash flow becomes an issue, they tend to cut back on services like yours without a second thought.

Cash flow isn't usually an issue for the bigger businesses, which means as long as you're doing a good job, they are in most cases happy to pay.

I spoke to a potential client recently who increased the overall life time value of his database of clients by three times, simply by only working with businesses who had a multimillion pound turnover.

Having a Niche

In all the years of working with some of the most successful Coaches, Trainers and Consultants one thing I've noticed is there are some that have defined their niche market, and have a clear picture of who it is they're marketing to, and there are others that tend to waiver or be unsure.

It's common for a Coach, Trainer or Consultant to view a niche market as narrowing their sales or cutting into a profit margin, so they fear it.

Some say *"We can Coach, Train or Consult for anyone in any position, - yep, regardless of the skill sets and experience required we can do it, after all Coaching, Training and Consultancy is Coaching, Training and Consultancy isn't it?"*

The truth is, having a well-defined niche market could be defined as a component that gives you business power. A niche market allows you to define who you're marketing to. It makes your message more powerful and specific. Something we'll look at in more detail later on.

When you know who you're marketing to, it's easy to determine where your marketing energy and funds should be spent. Quite frankly, unless you have the marketing budget of, say, Coca Cola or Ford motoring company, you simply cannot afford to market to everyone.

You see, once you have a well-defined niche, it is also *easier* to market to that niche because your communication will be specific to *their needs* and not general, as when you're communicating to the whole business community.

Your Dream 100 Clients

You see, I've been reading a book called the *'Ultimate Sales Machine'* by Chet Holmes, I highly recommend reading it if you haven't already done so.

One of the many client attraction strategies Chet talks about in the book is the *'Dream 100.'*

The *'Dream 100'* is a list you put together of your ideal clients and I'm talking about the crème de la crème here.

> ➤ The clients who have the finances available to pay for your most premium service...

> ➤ The clients who you enjoy serving the most...

> ➤ The clients who right now, seem completely out of your reach and are only available to you in your dreams...

Occasionally you can stumble across these dream clients almost by chance. You get lucky and one or two happen to cross the path of your business.

Everyone needs a little bit of luck once in a while, but it's much better to rely on a proven strategy for attracting this type of client. That's where the *'Dream 100'* comes in.

Chet Homes talks about how you can identify these 'dream clients' and then put together a marketing campaign that targets them directly and is specifically aimed at them and their needs.

The result?

You attract more of your dream clients, making you much closer to building that dream business. It's one of the most effective strategies that you can implement as a Coach, Trainer or Consultant!

Why Is 'The Dream 100' So Important To My Business Profits?

Chet Homes believes that this strategy has single handedly helped more companies double their sales faster than any other single concept, and it all comes down to something called the 80/20 Rule.

If you're unfamiliar with the 80/20 rule, let me explain in a bit more detail;

The 80/20 Rule, also known as 'Pareto Principle' and 'The Law of the Vital Few', encapsulates the TWO most important numbers in this or any other universe: 80 and 20.

It essentially sums up a general principle that in any system a majority of the outputs are a function of a minority of inputs, with the split often being 80/20 (meaning 80% of the outputs come from just 20% of the inputs).

As a Coach, Trainer or Consultant, it specifically means:

1. 80% of your sales come from just 20% of your marketing.

2. 80% of your profits come from just 20% of your services.

3. 80% of your problems come from just 20% of your clients.

4. 20% of your clients are responsible for 80% of your profits.

Now the numbers might not be exactly 80/20 (it might be 60/40 or 70/30 or even 99/1), but they ARE there.

So how do you use the 80/20 rule to become more effective?

It's simple, you focus more of your time and energy on the activities with the most output.

For example:

If 80% of your sales come from 20% of your activity that means that 80% of your activity only leads to 20% of your sales. Spend more time on the high output activities and you will make more sales with less work!

If 80% of your profits come from 20% of your clients spend more time and energy with the 20% of your clients that are worth the most to you.

If 80% of your problems come from 20% of your clients, get rid of that 20% of your clients and get rid of 80% of your problems.

In Chet Holmes' words:

"There are always a smaller number of 'best buyers' than there are "all buyers". The "best buyers" are the 20% of your potential clients that will make up 80% of your profits."

These clients are worth more to you in revenue, so if we focus our energy on getting more of them, then the profits will follow! And if all that wasn't enough to convince you, it's also cheaper to market to these guys as well!

You see, marketing to a smaller list of say 100 'best buyers' will cost you less in time and money than marketing to a bigger list of 1000 'all buyers.'

So you save money on your marketing and get bigger profits for it.

Best buyers buy more, buy faster and buy more often than any other buyers. These are your ideal clients to work with!

The Snow Ball Effect

"When best buyers buy, other best buyers buy faster."

The best thing about the 'Dream 100' strategy is that it doesn't lose effectiveness over time, instead, the more you use it, the more effective it becomes because of social proof.

You see, the 'best buyers' in all industries tend to follow suit. All the potential clients in your Dream 100 will have a similar network of contacts and you can use this to your advantage using what is known as 'Social Proof'.

Let's say your Dream 100 consists of some of the corporate banks for example. Saying to one corporate bank, that you also work with, or are speaking to another corporate bank, will only encourage them to take you more seriously.

I'm obviously far too young to remember, but it wasn't that long ago that it was frowned upon to live with your partner without being married to them first, and to have a child out of wedlock was even more frowned upon.

Today, with the exception of a few, people tend to live with their significant other before they marry. Celebrities and Hollywood stars were the first to break this taboo, paving the way for the rest of society to follow in their footsteps.

This is 'Social Proof' in action and you can use it in your business to boost your profits.

So, to sum this bit up...

One of the main reasons it's important to clearly define *"Who"* you target is because it should directly influence *"How"* you market your business. It's important to know who you're trying to reach, what attracts them, what piques their interest, what persuades them, and how they prefer to be offered and receive information.

It sounds obvious when you think about it, but you would be surprised at how many Coaches, Trainers and Consultants focus their marketing on what their service/product does and not what their client wants!

Most the marketing I see from Coaches, Trainers and Consultants is very broad, vague and generic, not narrow, focused and specific.

When you think about the typical non-direct-response advertising you see from the majority of the Coaches, Trainers and Consultants, it's very focused on the company and the brand and not on the client.

This type of marketing tends to work for big blue chip organizations who can afford to spend millions on any one campaign at a time, but for you in your business it tends to get swallowed up, meaning you get ignored.

Dan Kennedy, the god father of marketing, sums this up best in his book *"No B.S. Direct Marketing"* where he refers to this as...

"Trying to influence the ocean with thimbles-full of water... When you have comparatively limited resources, you must deploy them very selectively"

He's spot on of course!

The moral of the story is this; get *very specific* about who it is you want to work with, *what you ideal client looks like*, how they behave, what their needs are and what their spending behaviours are. and then craft a marketing message that meets those needs...

2. Message: Your opening Line

"Marketing and Sales isn't about trying to persuade, coerce, or manipulate people into buying your services. It is about putting yourself out in front of, and offering your services to those whom you are meant to serve - people who already need and are looking for your service."
Michael Port

The majority of Coaches, Trainers and Consultants I speak to don't particularly enjoy the 'marketing' side of things and so will try to avoid it as best they can.

But the truth is you're putting out marketing messages all the time whether you like it or not!

People will ask you *"what do you do?"* and you answer them without giving it too much thought.

You invest time and money into marketing your business via more traditional routes like the telephone, email and direct mail and you communicate with your current clients on a regular basis too.

All of this communication forms a part of your marketing message and there are *five things* you must know in order to make sure this communication is more effective next time around.

➤ Your clients and potential clients are bombarded by

communication just like this from your competitors and countless other competing businesses.

- ➤ Most communication that is designed to grab the attention of your potential clients fails miserably and gets ignored.

- ➤ Communication about you and the services you offer are a lot more interesting to you than they are to your potential clients.

- ➤ To get the attention of your clients and potential clients you need to talk about things that interest them.

- ➤ All your clients really care about are themselves, their problems and how to solve them.

Drill these five points into your way of thinking and you'll immediately see better results from your marketing.

One of my clients is a Business Coach and helps business owners get better results in their business including sales, team performance and overall business growth. When people asked him what he did, he used to just say *"I'm a Business Coach"*.

I remember him telling me that he could almost see people lose interest the moment he began the sentence... Even though he was sure the service he offered could help them solve the problem that they had in their business...

Nowadays when people ask the question, instead of just saying *"I'm a Business Coach"*, he Says: *"I work with Business Owners who want to increase their sales, improve the performance in their team and increase business profits..."* As you can probably imagine, rather than people losing interest, a response like this encourages the potential clients to press for more information because you're speaking directly to their needs!

And I can give you dozens of examples just like this where Coaches, Trainers and Consultants have tweaked how they communicate to clients and see a massive difference in the response they get.

Why should your clients buy from you?

One of the many questions I ask Coaches, Trainers and Consultants is *"What's your USP?"* and *"What can you offer your client that will give them peace of mind?"*

More often than not, the Coach, Trainer or Consultant thinks that the USP is some kind of skin disease, or they will explain that because they're independent, they're more flexible, care about the client... blah, blah, blah.

How having a *Unique Selling Proposition* (USP) will increase your sales

The Unique Selling Proposition (USP) is the number one thing that needs to be created before continuing with any other marketing endeavour. The USP is a statement or message that explains to your customers, one at a time, why they should buy from you.

The following is a list of reasons why you must have a USP in order to make your business prosper. One of our clients reported a *19% improvement* in conversion once their USP was implemented and communicated to potential clients.

Reasons why:

➲ 95% of Coaches, Trainers and Consultants do not understand what a USP is, or do not have an adequate USP. Therefore, if you DO have a successful USP, then you're ahead of 95% of all your competitors.

➲ Your competition may be reading this right now. If you do nothing about your USP, and your competitor does, guess who wins the most sales?

➲ The days of the all-inclusive business are gone. There is so much choice for consumers these days, you have to show them why they should buy from you, before they walk across the street and buy from the business that does clearly state what they do!

➲ If there are two Coaches, Trainers or Consultants (or worse three to five) that offer exactly the same thing in one geographical area, and the customer cannot distinguish between the two, one of them is redundant and will eventually fold. Just look around you and see the Coaches, Trainers and Consultants that come and go because they have failed to tell the customer why they should buy from them.

➲ You do not want to compete on price. Some Coaching, Training and Consultancy businesses get into the price war model where they all offer a commodity, and the only thing they have to compete with is price. Over time, you cannot sustain a business that competes on price alone. Someone will always come by and do it cheaper. If you craft your USP correctly, you can charge more than your competitors and still gain customers.

If you're happy with your sales growth and do not want to add a single customer to your list, then continue doing what you're doing. If you're looking to outsmart the competition, possibly triple your sales in a small amount of time and not have to add a penny to your marketing efforts, *then the USP is the way to go.*

For some Coaches, Trainers or Consultants if you're new or not sure of your niche this can be challenging.

Over the past few sections of this book I've been talking about your target audience and your message and that's no coincidence. You see, after speaking to and working with some of the world's top performing Coaches, Trainers and Consultants.... Every working marketing system I've ever come across or put together for my clients has been based on what's known as the *'Message-Market-Media Triangle'*

And this isn't based on solely my experience either. Speak to anyone that knows even the first thing about direct response marketing in any industry and they'll tell you the same thing and give you even more examples to back up my point.

This is the marketing tripod that supports your business if you will. No one element is more important than the other. They all hold equal importance and if one or more of the elements isn't working then your whole business falls apart.

There are eight possible ways this tripod can be formed;

1. Right Message – Wrong Market – Right Media

2. Right Message – Right Market – Wrong Media

3. Right Message – Wrong Market –Wrong Media

4. Wrong Message – Right Market –Right Media

5. Wrong Message –Wrong Market –Right Media

6. Wrong Message –Right Market –Wrong Media

7. Wrong Message –Wrong Market –Wrong Media

But there's one way and one way only to get it right and have your clients magnetically drawn towards you...

8. Right Message –Right Market – Right Media

And all three parts must work in sync with one another otherwise you'll be leaving money on the table, which leads us to the *third principle of seduction*;

3. Media: How to reach your 'Type'

Media refers to what communication method you use, to get your message to your market. And the list of options is endless.

To name just a few you've got: telemarketing, letters, newspapers, magazines, radio, postcards, email, websites, television and then online there seems to be a new method born every minute!

Here, your options are endless.

One of the questions I often get asked by the Coaches, Trainers and Consultants that I come across is: *"Which one works best?"*

And it's never a simple answer.

*Which one works best for you will depend entirely on
who your market is.*

Just to give you a basic example. Let's say you're selling a cure for blindness, and your target market is blind people between the ages of 25-40. It would probably be no use placing your advert in the newspaper because they wouldn't be able to see it, but the radio? That might work better...

The opposite is true if you're selling a cure for people that are hard of hearing.

The rule is to find ways to use as many different forms of media as you can. Where most Coaches, Trainers and Consultants go wrong, is that they become lazily dependent on only one, two or sometimes three methods for communicating with potential clients, be it telemarketing, networking or word of mouth.

Relying on so few, you're exposed to sudden business disruption or the entry of more aggressive competition.

Think about it, all else being equal. If you're just using one or two forms of media to reach your potential clients and a competitor or another professional in your field enters the market using six or seven. Who do you think is going to win the most business?

A More Detailed Look At Media

1.   Direct Mail

You have options, so first consider your budget and discover your options with the help of your coach and a mailing company.

Next, think about the objective for your client contact. Do you want to focus on a limited-time discount on a service or offer of a report/eBook?

With such a targeted focus, a postcard or flyer with punchy copy would suffice.

One of my clients specializes in coaching accountants. She will send out postcards offering a free eBook such as, 'How to grow your accountancy practice.'

For every 1000 postcards she sends out, she will get 20 requests for the eBook, and of those 20, at least one of them will lead to a client, and the others she nurtures over time, another three will sign up within 12 weeks.

Let's do the calculation on this formula.

To send 1000 post cards at 50p per card, equates to £500. Each one of her clients is worth £6000 in fees. So in theory, each campaign of 1000 post cards generates £24,000 (Four new clients x £6000), over the life time of the client.

2.   E-Shots (Email)

This is a very similar technique to the direct mailing mentioned above. Again offering the eBook and then nurturing.

The two main differences are, first of all there is no cost to getting the eShot out. However, it is worth remembering that the opening rates can be as low as 15%. Consequently if you send out a 1000 emails, only 150 of these emails actually get opened and read. If we work on the same percentage that requested the eBook from the direct mail, that's 3 requesting the book.

Of course the secret here is to email to a larger number, thus increasing your return.

3.   Search Engine Pay Per Click

Pay Per Click is an Online marketing model used to direct traffic to websites, where you pay the hosting service (such as Google, or Bing) when the advert is clicked. The beauty of this is you only pay when someone clicks on your advert. You can also set a weekly budget and once that has been met, then the advertising stops. This means you're controlling your marketing spend.

Pay Per Click is a great way to drive targeted prospects to your website, but in order for this to work, you need to test and measure results to make sure you're getting a return on your investment.

The way it works is that users go to the big search engines such as Google or Bing. And if what they're searching for matches your targeting options, your ad will be displayed. E.G. If someone searches the term "Business Consultant In New York" and you've targeted that search phrase with your ad. Your ad will be displayed to that user.

4.   Social Media (LinkedIn, Twitter and Facebook)

In my opinion, Social Media can be a waste of time if used in the wrong way. Saying that, there are some very powerful strategies that have worked for me and in the businesses of my clients. Before I go on, I want to remind you of one of the golden rules of marketing that I touched on in an earlier chapter; everything you do on social media must be to get a direct response from the client.

To implement a successful Social Media marketing strategy takes little financial investment. However, it does require relentless time commitment, not only to make it work, but to maximize its effectiveness. And time is money! So before you dive into social media head first, be sure you're investing your time in the right area,

In order to be successful, you need to keep up with and manage your effort over time, without neglecting other important areas of your business.

In order to be a successful marketer, you need to engage your audience and communicate with them through several mediums. Social Media allows you to do this, whilst building your network and directing targeted traffic to your website and landing pages.

Once you have successfully implemented this marketing strategy into your business, you can expect to generate an additional ten to fifteen leads per month, every month, just by using this route to market alone!

Before you begin, you need to know that there are literally hundreds of social media platforms out there, so it's important to only invest your time in the ones that get you the best results.

Our research has found that there are currently *three social media sites that give Coaches, Trainers or Consultant the best return in terms of time invested.*

✓ LinkedIn

✓ Twitter

✓ Facebook

LinkedIn

LinkedIn is the world's largest professional network with over 227 million members and growing rapidly. LinkedIn connects you to your trusted contacts and helps you exchange knowledge, ideas, and opportunities with a broader network of professionals.

Let me ask you a question.

Since there are 227 million members on LinkedIn, do you think it is possible that your potential clients are on there waiting to hear from you?

You see I work with a number of top performing Coaches, Trainers and Consultants who only use LinkedIn to attract clients.

Here is an example of generating leads through LinkedIn:

One of my clients works in the energy conservation sector. So he created a group on LinkedIn for professionals on that sector. In less than three months he was the owner of the largest group in that sector on LinkedIn. He sends his group members high value content every month. He drives them to his website to get the material, and guess what, every month at least 4 potential clients ask if he can contact them regarding small business.

Twitter

Twitter is a website, owned and operated by Twitter Inc., which offers a social networking and micro blogging service, enabling its users to send and read messages called tweets. Tweets are based on text posts of up to 140 characters.

Some interesting facts about Twitter according to – www.digitalbuzzblog.com

- There are over 106 million active Twitter accounts
- The number of Twitter users increases by approximately 300,000 per day
- Twitter users are sending over 55 million tweets per day

So, imagine if just 0.01% of Twitter users were in your target market. If one of your competitors implemented Twitter into their marketing strategy and you didn't. Who do you think would generate the most leads, communicate to the most prospects and sign the most clients?

Facebook

Some interesting facts about Facebook:

- There are more than 750 million active users
- 50% of our active users log on to Facebook in any given day
- People spend over 700 billion minutes per month on Facebook

So what do these interesting facts and figures mean to you as a

Coach, Trainer or Consultant? To put it quite simply, there are a mass of potential clients waiting to hear from you on these social media platforms, with the added benefit that it is relatively easy to target your niche.

If you're not currently using social media, in my opinion you're losing out on revenue for your business. You see marketing is very much a numbers game. The more people you communicate to, the more leads you'll get and the more clients you'll acquire. Social Media is a great, cost-effective way to communicate to your target market.

One thing that all these Social Media sites have in common is their 'Display Advertising' interface. You can now use the information these sites have collected about it's users to precision target your ads to reach them. For example using LinkedIn you can target people within a certain geographical area, who have a certain job title and who are of a certain age. A Very powerful tool for those willing to look into it.

5. Remarketing

Remarketing is a feature that lets you reach clients who have previously visited your website, but did not take the action you wanted them to take.

You can now show them relevant adverts across the web or when they search on Google. When people leave your site without engaging with you, remarketing helps you connect with these potential clients again. You can even show them a tailored message or offer that will encourage them to return to your site and request further information or contact you.

Use remarketing to match the right message to the right people at the right time. Here's how: You add a piece of code or 'cookie' to all of the pages of your site. Then, when a client comes to your site, they'll be added to your remarketing lists. You can later connect with these potential buyers while they search on Google or browse other websites.

From the client's point of view, it seems that you're everywhere. The best bit is, if you do it on Pay per `click you only pay if they're interested and click on your advert.

Many companies are using this right now, and more and more Coaching, Training and Consultancy companies are enjoying huge success with this method.

One of our clients reported a 33% increase in 'opt-in' conversion when they implemented this into their marketing.

6.   Joint Venture/Strategic Allegiance Host Beneficiary

This method is considered one of the most powerful ways to attract warm leads, when you and your business implement this system and systemize the procedure you'll have:

- ✓ More clients
- ✓ Generate more income
- ✓ Increase turnover
- ✓ Have greater security for you and your family.

This method of lead generation has been a marketing method for holiday companies, mail order companies, newspapers and magazines and numerous on-line businesses.

A Joint Venture takes on many forms, such as asking a company that sells to the same market as you, if they would email their list informing their clients of your service. In return the company will expect some form of reimbursement typically a percentage of invoice value, or a reciprocal arrangement.

Whatever deal you agree, whenever you approach a 'host' company you should endeavour to extend a special offer to his/her clients. This maybe in the form of extended warranty, free bonus or even reduced price.

Why Joint Ventures work so well:

Have you ever called a cold prospect? It can be at times tedious and some of my clients find it nerve-racking at the thought of rejection.

Joint Ventures allow you leverage off the credibility of others.

Did you know it is 500% easier to get an existing client to buy than it is to persuade a new client to purchase?

It positions the host in a positive light. The business owner is recommending a service that benefits his/her clients, and the clients appreciate that he/she is looking out for them.

You can reciprocate and generate money for your business.

It is virtually risk free.

One of my clients recently bought a Coaching franchise and with the monthly investment he has to make to the franchise owner, it was imperative his business hit the ground running.

Well the first thing he did was get himself a coach to ensure that he did what he said he was going to do. He explained to me that he had no database of potential clients and wanted the fastest and most effective method for growing his small business. I shared with him the *"Don't sell to people, sell through people"* mantra.

Let me explain. He arranged meetings with 23 accountancy firms in his town and then made the following offer to them:

"I will coach you completely free for six months; on the understanding that once you see how this benefits you, you'll then introduce my Coaching firm to your B2B (Business to Business) clients." Of the 43 he spoke to, seven took up the offer immediately.

Look at it from the accountant's point of view, they have nothing to lose. This coach went from zero income to £180k pa in 12 months, using only that method. In his second year he took on two other coaches, as he was unable to cope with the leads he was getting. Again none of his team ever makes a cold call.

7. The Systemized Referral Process System

When you have this in place, properly in place, then you'll get some remarkable benefits. To start with you can obtain hundreds, yes, hundreds of low cost or even 'no cost' leads.

Referrals tend to have a higher conversion rate than any other type of lead.

- ✓ You have satisfied customers. People only provide referrals when they're satisfied with the products and services they're receiving.

- ✓ You'll experience increased turnover and profits and whatever benefits you get as a result of those increases.

- ✓ You'll acquire assignments through the referral route rather than through cold sales.

- ✓ You'll have the opportunity to reduce your marketing spend.

- ✓ You'll lock in current clients to you.

- ✓ You'll have reduced acquisition cost per customer.

These are some of the great benefits from getting referrals and the only real way to do it, to get all of these advantages, is to have a systemized process.

Without a doubt, referrals can be the least expensive capture cost leads we ever receive.

Often, referrals can be obtained at no cost. However, should a cost be associated, it would be on a contingency basis. That is, payment would only be necessary for converted business or new clients and not just for the leads.

Earlier I mentioned that a lot of Coaches, Trainers and Consultants often say they get the business via 'word of mouth/referral.' However when you dig deeper, we often discover that they have not systemized the process and they get very few.

Here is an example from a Consultancy Firm owner who works only with blue chip organizations such as Proctor and Gamble and other FMCG organizations.

Due to the nature of the business his company does, he tends to work with the sales director and sales manager. He has incorporated a very simple system that means once an assignment has been completed, and the client is extremely satisfied, He asks them a series of very precise questions. Each time he does this he gets between 4-10 leads!

His conversion rate is 8% (that maybe needs working on) each client is worth £8000 p.a. and over a lifetime about £40,000. He has a thriving small business that turns over in excess of £750,000 per year. By simply asking the right questions to the right people.

Parthenon

You may remember during an earlier section of this book I mentioned that one of the golden rules of marketing is that *"the worst number in your business is one"*?

This couldn't be more relevant than when it comes to the media you use to communicate to your potential clients.

At this point I'd like to share with you an experience I once had with one of my very first clients. Rachel her name is... A really nice lady based on the other side of the world in sunny Australia...

She had been in business for about five years, was great at what she does and ALWAYS gets the best results for her clients.... But guess what?

Her business was hanging by a thread!

Why?

She only had one way of bringing in new business. Which worked 'OK' for her for the most part.

But... When she has a bad month or even worse a few bad months, and that method of bringing in business doesn't perform as well as it usually does. Her business really suffered... Massively! And what would happen?

All of a sudden its panic stations! She starts to feel insecure because she doesn't know where her next paycheck is coming from, she loses confidence in what she offers meaning her sales conversions start to drop. She feels stressed because it now means she has to work EVEN harder for the coming months just so she can make up the short fall and this means she is not on top form to deliver the best results for the clients she already has...

Imagine having your ONLY profit source swept from under your feet in a flash. Leaving you on your backside wondering where it all went wrong...

The problem with only having one way of bringing business in is that if, for whatever reason, that particular method doesn't perform as well as it normally does. You lose out big time. Your business is literally being supported by a single pillar and if it falls, down comes your entire empire and your profits crash down with it.

To protect yourself against this happening to you. Each and every month, test and implement at least one new route to market. Some will work wonders, some won't work at all, but that's just part of business. Continuously adding new methods of bringing in clients will not only mean that if one underperforms you have plenty of others to fall back on... it will also have a massive impact on your business revenue and growth. The goal is to have your business profits supported by a Parthenon, rather than a single pillar.

4. Irresistible Offer: Get Their Interest

Your "irresistible offer" is designed to get a new prospect to step forward, indicating an interest gives you permission and invitation to sell to them, this is often done by creating and offering 'information' of relevance to what you sell and of interest to the prospect.

Most Coaches, Trainer and Consultants have a version of this concept in the shape of a free consultation, free coaching session or even just by offering to buy the potential client lunch.

But although an offer like the above may seem irresistible on the inside, from the client point of view all they really hear is:

"I have to spend an hour maybe two with this person I don't really know that well, who's probably going to ask me all sorts of personal questions about my business, who might not even be able to help me because my problem is unique, and who at the end of it is going to try to sell to me..."

All of a sudden, your no risk irresistible offer for a free consultation turns into the clients' worst nightmare.

Let's imagine you're a sales trainer. Rather than trying to get them to meet with you right from the off - what we're essentially saying is this.

If you have a problem with the sales in your team. That is a problem I can help you fix. But I'm also aware you have no way of knowing that and therefore no reason to trust that I can get you the results I say I can. So before I try and sell to you I first want to begin the relationship by offering you this free book called "10 Things To Do To Increase The Sales In Your Team"

You have lots of options when it comes to creating an 'irresistible offer'. It can be a book, a video series, a free report, a webinar. You have lots of options. It just needs to be low risk in the eyes of the potential client.

5. Lead Capture: Get their details.

In order for you to be able to track the prospects who have responded to your irresistible offer. You need a means of 'lead capture' or 'response'. This is just a case of you gathering as much contact information about that particular prospect as you can. For example: in order for them to get your free PDF report of improving sales, you need their name and email address etc.

We'll look more at this part of the process in the *Internet Marketing* section in chapter seven.

6. Short Term Follow Up: Nurturing the relationship

My theory is, most kids have this step mastered by the age of two!

Don't believe me?

I remember baby-sitting for my two-year-old brother some years back. He struggled to walk in straight lines most of the time; he was probably amongst the top 5 messiest eaters in the world and has the attention span of... well, a two year old!

But anyone that's been 'fortunate' enough to spend even a short amount of time with any two year old that can form the sentence *"Can I have some chocolate?"* knows the power of relentless follow up!

Did you know that only 2% of your prospects actually make a buying decision after just the first contact?

The problem is, if you're like most Coaches, Trainers and Consultants and you don't follow up enough with prospects, you're leaving 98% of your business profits on the table for someone else to take.

How long can you afford to keep doing that for?

This step in this process is all about following up with your prospects and should carry with it a second 'irresistible offer' that's linked to whatever next step you want the prospect to take.

For example, here is where you may want to offer that chance of a free one- on-one consultation with you. At this stage of the process they know who you are, you know they have a problem and they know you have at least some expertise when it comes to solving it. There is a lot less risk from the potential client's point of view at this stage compared to in the beginning.

7. Long Term Follow Up: Lead Maintenance

The Seventh principle is a mirror of step Six just over a longer period. It's maintenance of leads to catch the ones that perhaps didn't respond first time around. Step Seven is endless and essentially continues until the potential client either "buys, dies, or unsubscribes"

In step Six, we talked about the importance of 'follow up' in order to get your prospects to know, like and trust you...

But let's take a slightly different look ... follow up is also so important because there are other reasons people don't respond, even when they DO like and trust you.

Here are just a few reasons why even your most seasoned and loyal followers might not respond immediately and why you need to keep reminding them:

1. They didn't get your message last time.

2. They got it, but didn't read it.

3. Maybe they were in a bad mood.

4. Last week they didn't need your services, this week they do.

See, there are LOTS of reasons they don't say "yes" that have absolutely nothing to do with them saying "no" and everything to do with them simply being completely oblivious.

I'm reminded of the gentleman who engaged the services of my client. After taking the trouble to respond saying, "thank you for your offer, but I'm happy without any extra help and support".... He remained in step seven and eventually made contact a few weeks later saying, "I've decided to try your service as I really like your approach".

And THIS is why you shouldn't just send random marketing pieces, make a random cold-call or offer patchy promotion occasionally and then call it a day. THIS is why we have multi-step, multi-media campaigns. Because it's true, some people respond better to different mediums such as, email or direct mail and others respond better to a personal phone call.

And THIS is why Coaches, Trainers and Consultants who master the art of relationship building prosper and those who don't... DON'T!

Here's what we've covered during this chapter...

1. Market

2. Media

3. Message

4. Irresistible offer

5. Lead capture

6. Short term follow up

7. Long term follow up

Chapter 6
Influencing With Integrity – The Art
Of Relationship Building And Sales

Have you ever wondered why another Coach, Trainer or Consultant in exactly the same sector as you is growing business year on year? You constantly come up against them, in fact, they're probably your number one competitor, and it feels as if they have the edge as they always seem to get the business you're after.

There is a very good reason why that's happening and I'm going to share the secrets with you. When you read this section and commit to mastering the skills required, you'll make more sales, earn more money and work fewer hours.

Did you notice the caveat?

It's all very well reading this and thinking that's great, now I know what needs to be done to enjoy more success. However, if you do *nothing* with the information and keep doing what you have always done, you'll have what you always have had.

If you want to inspire others in your team, or if you simply want to discover how to influence with integrity and have fantastic relationships with friends, colleagues and clients read on.

The ability to influence is one of the most highly sought after skills, be it in business, to influence your clients or team, or perhaps at home with your partner and children. Studies have shown that individuals who are able to master the skill of influencing with integrity, are able to move up the corporate ladder quicker, have better relationships and generally seem to be happier. The ability to influence means that you get more clients, earn more money and have better relationships.

With the ability to influence, you're able to let others know what it is you want to accomplish. You have the ability to motivate and inspire others as well as resolve conflict.

Over the years, I have had the opportunity to work with some of the world's top performing Coaches, Trainers and Consultants. Modelled the techniques that work and I share them with you. I will also share with you techniques that have been discovered by social psychologists.

Over the years, we have all seen and heard masters in the art of influencing with integrity. I sometimes wonder what type of world we would live in without masters such as Nelson Mandela, Bill Gates, Margaret Thatcher, Ghandi, Winston Churchill and Martin Luther King.

Let me ask you, what type of life would you have if you mastered these techniques and could always influence with integrity?

Here are 7 tips to help you get started:

Tip #1. Remember the name of the person you get introduced to

Imagine the scene; you've just been introduced to one of the Directors of your largest client at a corporate event. As the day progresses you get an opportunity to share a drink with them. However, although you were introduced less than two hours before, you've forgotten their name! Tell me, do you think that matters? Of course it does. Just imagine that if every time you met someone you could commit their name to your memory forever.

Well you can by using these simple and effective techniques:

Commit – to remembering every person's name, make that decision now! If you have always told yourself you're lousy at remembering names – it's true. If you now tell yourself that you always remember names – it's true. Whatever you believe is true to you.

Concentrate – pay attention to the name that you're told. If you didn't hear it, ask them to repeat it. If you find the name unusual ask them to spell it to you. Better still, have a note pad with you and write the name down as it is spelt to you. As you're given the person's name get a clear and detailed picture of that person. Then imagine their name is written across their forehead. Note the person's physical characteristics. Use all your senses to form a lasting impression.

Repeat – Repetition helps engrave the name in your memory.

- ✓ Use the name silently to yourself
- ✓ Make a comment on the name if possible
- ✓ Use the name in conversation
- ✓ Use it when leaving

How successful would you be if you mastered this skill so well that it became second nature?

Tip #2. *"Seek first to understand then to be understood."* - Stephen Covey

When communicating, spend your time understanding what that person is saying and what they want. We all understand that in an ideal world our decisions are based on logic and sound reasoning. In the real world, people act in response to their personal preferences, feelings and social influences, and sometimes they're not even aware of it.

Find common ground. Listening is crucial to influencing with integrity, by demonstrating that your values, aspirations and concerns are the same as theirs. This shows that you can see things from their point of view and have empathy.

Tip # 3. Show you really care for the person that you want to influence.

This applies if you're at home or at work. When you show that you really care for the person that you're influencing, they're more likely to accept another point of view. Interestingly, when they believe you care about them, they're more likely to offer you more information, thus enabling you to influence them.

Tip # 4. How to never lose another argument

This technique is quite simple and has a 100% success rate.

DO NOT ARGUE WITH ANYONE AT ANY TIME!

It really is that simple. You may well win the argument, but that's all you're going to win. If you decide that you don't have to be right, you'll never argue again and that way you'll never lose an argument.

Tip #5. *"Begin with the end in mind."* - Stephen Covey

Begin with the end in mind when you start the conversation, negotiation or influencing. As simple as it sounds, it really is extremely effective. By knowing your desired outcome you can take the appropriate steps to get there. The most successful influencers do this every time.

Seek the win/win on every occasion. If you win and the client wins that's great. If either party believe that they have lost in some way, you're simply storing problems for later. By doing your research and understanding what is negotiable, you can offer something that's valuable.

Tip #6. There is a stereotypical image of a sales person

Often the term that's used is 'gift of the gab'. Whilst undoubtedly the ability to communicate effectively with clients and potential clients is important, what's even more important is to understand what the needs of the clients are.

Let me explain in more detail. All human beings are motivated to avoid pain and gain pleasure.

A client of mine who is a Coaching, Training and Consultancy consultant complained that whenever she visited clients they would sit on the fence about deciding who to use. I explained that what she needed to do was establish what the client's pain was regarding Coaching, Training and Consultancy .

The real skill is influencing in such a way so that your client wants to buy more from you than you want to sell to them.

Time and time again, business people have been taught about features, benefits and USP's (unique selling propositions). Whilst these do have a part in influencing your clients, the real skill is having the client wanting to buy from you more than you want to sell to them.

Please pay extra attention

It is easier to sell the avoidance of pain than it is to sell the gaining of pleasure.

You see away motivation is the catalyst for action, towards motivation is the continuation of action.

Psychologists have found this to be the most effective method for getting your clients to want to buy from you more than you want to sell.

Tip #7. Rapport

I'm sure you have been in a situation where you've met someone for the first time and afterwards you felt that you didn't like them or they weren't your kind of person. If I were to ask you why, usually you would have trouble explaining why that was. Equally, I'm sure you've met someone and within minutes you felt completely at ease with them.

I can assure you this is not coincidence. When you get on with someone you are in rapport with them. This creates a climate of trust and understanding which is vital for influencing. Psychologists have discovered precisely what needs to happen for you to be in rapport with someone, enabling you to trust and understand them and vice-versa.

Rapport is a form of influence. When you're communicating with someone, once you're in rapport, they will do all that they can to see your point of view. The quality of the rapport you have will influence the quality of influence. Interestingly, most of what's going on when you're in rapport with someone is happening unconsciously.

The Six Factors of Influence

"Here's where the emotional triggers come in."
Robert Cialdini

Researcher and author Robert Cialdini, describes the Six Weapons of Influence, (in his book, Influence: Science and Practice1) as reciprocation, commitment and consistency, social proof, liking, authority and scarcity. As these are such powerful 'weapons' I'm now going to share with you my take on these six influences.

1. RECIPROCATION - *"The Old Give and Take-and Take"*

All of us are taught that we should find some way to repay others for what they do for us. Most people will make an effort to avoid being considered a moocher, ingrate, or person who does not pay their debts.

This is an extremely powerful tactic and can even spur unequal exchanges. In one experiment, for example, half the people attending an art appreciation session were offered a soft drink. Afterwards, all were asked if they would buy 25-cent raffle tickets. Guess what? The people who had been offered the soft drinks purchased twice as many raffle tickets, whether or not they had accepted the drinks!

You probably already use this principle, but it's much stronger than you suspect. You can build a sense of indebtedness in someone by delivering a number of uninvited 'first favours" over time. They don't have to be tangible gifts. In today's world, useful information is one of the most valuable favours you can deliver.

One of the ethical ways in which you and I can use the power of reciprocation and obligation, is by providing free reports that help our potential client overcome a particular challenge. This is a brilliant way to expose our customers to our services and let them see for themselves how they can benefit. It also, as you will gather, includes the power of reciprocation.

Example:

One supermarket used this idea, with a slight twist, when selling cheese. Rather than just offering samples, it allowed customers to cut their own piece of cheese, this created far greater sales than they had ever experienced before.

What are the other ways in which you can provide free samples for your customers?

Unfortunately, or perhaps fortunately, dependent upon the business in which you're involved, uninvited gifts work just as well. I'm certain you've received direct mail that includes free pens, coins or even Christmas cards, all designed to utilize the power of obligation and reciprocation.

Now there's a very important point here - the repayment of the obligation doesn't always equal the first favour. Someone may provide a very small favour for you and you may repay it with value far exceeding that first favour.

2. COMMITMENT AND CONSISTENCY - *"Hobgoblins of the Mind."*

We all have the desire to be consistent and appear as consistent human beings, this can work for and against us. We take actions that are consistent with previous actions and — importantly — we take action based on previously expressed beliefs.

Everyone uses shortcut decision-making processes in so many different areas of their lives.

Example: Let me share with you some fascinating information from Cialdini's book:

Some researchers in America went to people's houses and asked them to agree to put a large billboard in their front gardens regarding road safety. The billboard was ugly and badly designed.

As you might expect 83% refused and only 17% agreed (though from the way in which Cialdini describes the billboard I'm surprised that even 17% agreed).

So the researchers tested a different strategy.

They went to another set of houses and asked the owners if they would be prepared to put a three-inch square sign in their front windows, which said, 'Be a safe driver!' As you can imagine, most said, "Yes."

Then, a couple of weeks later, the researchers went back and asked the people who had previously agreed to the three-inch sign, if they would be prepared to have the ugly billboard in their front gardens and amazingly, or perhaps not so, 76% agreed.

Not only is this fascinating information, the fact that 76% said yes, but you and I can use this idea with integrity, to increase sales conversion rates, and thereby increase turnover and profits.

Once people have made a choice or taken a stand, they're under both internal and external pressure to behave consistently with that commitment. This desire for consistency offers us all a shortcut to action as we recall a previous decision we have already made.

When you can get someone to commit verbally to an action, the chances go up sharply that they'll actually do it. For example, before starting your next meeting, ask each person to commit to following the posted agenda. Then, if anyone goes off on a tangent, just ask them to explain how it fits the agenda. If they can't, they'll quickly fall back in line.

When we are asked to take further actions, that are totally in alignment, with those previously expressed beliefs, we will use shortcut decision- making processes and take congruent action.

So how do you and I use this knowledge?

Well, during the gathering stage of your business development meeting, you need to find out the beliefs and values of your customers, regarding the product or service you're selling. Then, provided that we are asking our customers to take action or actions that are in alignment with those beliefs and values, they're far more likely to say, "Yes!"

Example: Selling your Coaching, Training and Consultancy service

What questions can you ask that will have the customer telling you who they are?

"Do you use a Coaching, Training or Consultancy firm?"

The 'yes' — indicates that the customer already believes in the concept. The next question could be: "Why?" A simple 'Why?' would probably be too blunt, but the answer to this 'why' type question would have the customer telling you their beliefs and values about why they use a Coaching, Training and Consultancy firm, then you can capitalize on that statement about who they are.

Example questions;

"What is it about your current Coaching, Training and Consultancy service provider you would like to see more of?"

"What is it you would like to see less of?"

"If I could help you overcome the number one challenge."

I'm certain that you have the idea.

This is one of the most powerful ideas I can share with you. I urge you to take this thought, work with it and create a series of questions that will enable you to find out the beliefs and values of your potential customers so you can correctly align any actions you wish the customer to take with their stated position.

It's far easier for a customer to make a series of small decisions, rather than one BIG decision at the end of the sales conversation. Each question confirms their beliefs and values, both generally and specifically to the ideas you're putting forward.

3. SOCIAL PROOF - *"Truths Are Us"*

We decide what is correct by noticing what other people think is correct. This principle applies especially to the way we determine what constitutes the correct behaviour. If everyone else is behaving in a certain way, we assume that's the right thing to do. For example, one of the important, and largely unconscious ways we decide what's acceptable behaviour, on our current job, is by watching the people around us, especially the higher-ups or old-timers.

This principle of influence kicks in even more strongly when the situation is uncertain or people aren't sure what to do. When you can show them what others like them believe, or are doing, people are more likely to take the same action. The mass suicides among the Heavens Gate followers in Southern California and the people in Jonestown are horrible examples of the negative power of this principle.

On the positive side, product endorsements are the most obvious application of social proof. If you want someone to do something for you, be sure to let them see that many other people are already doing it, or are willing to do it. Show them that others like them (and the more like them the better) believe in your product or are using it.

Let me give you some examples of how social proof prompts people to take action, and then suggest how you can use it in your various sales and business activities.

To start with, I'm sure that you've seen, as I have, the growth of testimonials in direct mail and on websites, often accompanied by a photograph of the person giving the testimonial, together with their comment, full name and even their address or contact numbers (just having the first name could make your readers question the credibility).

That's social proof; an endorsement by others that the product or service on offer has been tried by other people and works so well for them that they're prepared to state that fact publicly, and even be photographed with the product and their positive comment about it.

Often, when we start working with clients, there is some reluctance to do this for fear of telling their competitors who they're working with, but when you realize that when a client gives you a testimonial, it helps cement the relationship, and the client is unlikely to go elsewhere, does it matter?.

Lastly, try and get as many testimonials as possible, as those in the audience who are being exposed to the opportunity for the first time will hopefully be able to identify with at least one person who has given a testimonial. And will therefore be saying to themselves, "If they can do it and they're like me... then I can probably do it too!"

This is the power of social proof.

4. LIKING - *"The Friendly Thief"*

People love to say 'yes' to requests from people they know and like. And people tend to like others who appear to have similar opinions, personality traits, background, or lifestyle. More people will say 'yes' to you if they like you, and the more similar to them you appear to be, the more likely they are to like you.

Claldini discovered 4 Key Factors in the Liking Principle.

The 4 Key Factors in the liking principle:

1. Physical attractiveness
2. Similarity
3. Compliments
4. Familiarity

Physical Attractiveness

When people are attractive to us we credit them with other positive characteristics — this is called the 'Halo Effect'. Because they're attractive to us we also tend to believe that they're honest, that they have high integrity and that what they say is believable.

So whilst attractiveness is in the eye of the beholder, it is up to you and I to do our best to look our best at all times. One piece of research even indicated that juries gave lighter fines to attractive defendants. Is it any wonder then that defendants are coached by their lawyers, and dressed to impress?

Similarity

This is similarity in:

- Opinions
- Dress
- Background
- Lifestyle
- Recreational activities.

Basically everything!

What can you find out about potential business partners or customers that you have in common? This builds rapport or Liking!

One simple way to create similarity is in dress. If a potential customer is in shirtsleeves, then it would make sense for you to remove your jacket.

Compliments

When people pay us compliments we like them, it's that simple!

Most people are also phenomenal suckers for flattery, even when they know it isn't true. When we have a good opinion of ourselves, we can accept praise and like those who provide it. Those with low self-esteem reject even well-earned praise and distrust the source. All salespeople worth their salt have mastered the flattery tactic. They know it works, but they may not know why.

However, here's a thought for you; when paying compliments, don't compliment the person, compliment the action. Compliments of the person sound like flattery; compliments of the action and result sound far more sincere, which of course they should be.

Familiarity

We tend to say, *"yes"* more easily to people with whom we have regular contact, in a positive environment, which is why social days with clients can work so well. Days at sporting events, days at the races, going to the theatre, almost anything.

People also tend to like and trust anything familiar. The best way to build this familiarity is to have frequent, pleasant contacts. For example, if you spend three hours straight with someone you've never met before, you would get a sense of who they are. But if you divided the same time into 30-minute segments of pleasant interaction over six consecutive weeks, you would each have a much stronger and positive knowledge about the other. You have established a comfort level, familiarity, and a history with them. Their repeated pleasant contacts with your organization's services or products helps builds familiarity and liking.

5. AUTHORITY - *"Directed Deference"*

Most of us are raised with a respect for authority, both real and implied. Sometimes, people confuse the symbols of authority (titles, appearance, possessions) with the true substance.

Some people are more strongly influenced by authority than others, and compliance can vary according to the situation. For example, it's 11:00 p.m., and the doorbell rings. Two men in police uniforms want to come in and ask you some questions. Most people respect such authority enough that they would comply, even though the Constitution says they don't have to. But if it was 3:00 a.m. and the men were in street clothes, claiming to be detectives, most of us would hesitate. The men would have to overcome our resistance with more proof of their authority, like badges or a search warrant.

You can put this general principle to use by citing authoritative sources to support your ideas. Look and act like an authority yourself. Be sure others know that your education and experience supports your ideas. Dress like the people who are already in the positions of authority that you seek.

There are three main factors of authority:

1. Titles
2. Clothes
3. Trappings.

Titles

    Doctor
    Professor
    Director
    Manager

One man even reported in Cialdini's book that he didn't use his title of professor with new people, as the conversations were too dull, and they treated him with too much respect.

Can you use an appropriate title?

Clothes

One study showed that 3% more people followed a researcher onto a busy road when wearing a suit compared to when he was dressed casually.

It's essential in business and selling to wear the appropriate clothes, ones that state your authority.

Trappings

These include your desk, your car, your briefcase.

All of these state your authority. Authority figures are believed and when they're believed, people take action and compliance rates rise.

So be careful when dealing with those who appear to have authority — is the authority figure really an expert? Use these ideas with integrity when selling and having business meetings.

6. SCARCITY - *"The Rule of the Few"*

Nearly everyone is vulnerable to some form of the principle of scarcity. Opportunities seem more valuable when they're less available. Hard-to-get things are perceived as better than easy-to-get things. For example, the object you've almost decided to buy is out of stock. The salesperson offers to check their other stores. And guess what? A store across town has one left! Do you buy it? Of course!

Whenever appropriate, you can use the Scarcity Principle. Refer to limited resources and time limits to increase the perceived value of the benefits of helping or working with you. The possibility of losing something is a more powerful motivator than of gaining something. Let others (a customer, your boss, a lover) know what they will be losing if they don't say 'yes' to your offer.

Now here's a strange fact:

If people manage to obtain the item that's scarce, they will also believe that it's better than they would have believed if, the item had been in plentiful supply.

The scarcity principle even works with information. When someone believes they know a secret they will...

- ✓ Believe it
- ✓ Believe it more than normal
- ✓ Take action.

How can you use the scarcity principle in your business?

The Six Factors of Influence are *incredibly powerful* and can be combined in many ways. Use them whenever you approach people you want to influence (and be sure to read Professor Cialdini's book, Influence: Science, and Practice. you'll find it most entertaining as well enlightening).

Accelerated Sales Process in Action

I'm going to share some fascinating information with you that will enable you to increase sales and profits, by being more easily able to persuade other people to your point of view by expanding on the Six Factors of Influence we've just looked at.

Also, you're going to discover how to overcome the most common objections as to why the prospect will not work with you.

You'll also discover the 19 words that, when used before any business development meeting, will improve conversion by up to 25%.

Some of these ideas are taken from the book already mentioned (Influence: Science and Practice by Dr. Robert Cialdini). They're also taken from my own experiences of selling over many years, as well as those of other successful

Coaches, Trainers and Consultants.

The 3 basic ideas of influence:

1. Fixed Action Patterns
2. Triggers
3. Perceptual Contrast

Fixed Action Patterns

All human beings have a habitual way of responding to certain stimuli; let me give you some examples.

Fixed action example:

If someone puts out their right hand towards you, then you'll automatically respond by grasping their hand and shaking it. Your action has been automatically triggered by their action. If someone smiles at you, usually, though not always, you'll smile back.

So you can see from just this example, that as human beings we respond automatically to certain actions taken by others. This simple concept is extremely powerful in the art and science of persuasion.

This is why body language is so important in communication, because certain body language gestures will automatically trigger certain actions by other people.

As human beings, we are finely tuned receiving devices and will respond to particular words that people use along with the tonality of those words.

I'm certain that in your private life you've asked your partner or someone close to you:

"How are you?" And their response was, *"Yeah - I'm OK!"* You'll immediately know, by the tonality that they're not OK, and no doubt your facial expression changed into a questioning one and you responded with, *"Are you sure?"* It was an automatic response on your part.

Triggers

Now let's talk about other triggers: Price Perception. Cialdini gives an example where a jewellery store owner left a message for one of their staff to halve the price of some jewellery that simply wasn't moving. The member of staff misread the note and doubled the price. The jewellery was sold almost immediately.

Sometimes we are triggered to take action by the higher price of an item, rather than the lower price of an item.

We have a higher perception of value based on the higher price. This is because of shortcut decision-making, everyone uses it. As things become more complicated, we use more shortcut decisions.

Just think of the majority of the decisions you make in your life? They will mostly be based on previous experiences. They will be shortcuts. What triggers or shortcuts do you use, and would it be worth re-examining some of those decisions in the light of this information?

On the commercial front, this is one of the reasons that buyers continue to buy from the same source. Having once made a calculated decision, the original decision, they continue to use a shortcut decision-making process, because it's easier than having to rethink the whole deal.

Now that you have that information, how will you communicate to make your client want to use you?

The Perception of Contrast

I'll give you a classic example of how contrast works both for us and against us:

Imagine this situation; you have three buckets of water: The one on the left contains hot water. The one on the right contains cold water. And the one in the middle contains tepid water. You put your left hand in the left-hand bucket, the hot water. You put your right hand in the right-hand bucket, the cold water and then, after a few minutes when your hands have become accustomed to the different temperatures, you plunge both hands into the middle bucket (you'll recall that the middle bucket contains tepid water).

Now a strange thing happens - your left hand, which has been in the hot water, thinks the water in the middle bucket is cold; whereas your right hand, which has been in the cold water, thinks the water in the middle bucket is hot!

That's what's called the perception of contrast. So how do you and I use this in business?

Well, the first thing to note is, that it's always a good idea, when selling or negotiating, to mention the highest-priced item first. Then, any subsequently-mentioned items would seem lower by contrast.

Here's what we've covered during this chapter...

1. Reciprocation

2. Commitment & consistency

3. Social Proof

4. Liking

5. Authority

6. Scarcity

Chapter 7
Why The Internet Can Be Your Very Own Personal Goldmine

The Internet is an information highway. When your prospects want answers or solutions, the first point of call is the Internet.

Think about how you use the big search engines like Google, Yahoo and Bing. We use the Internet to get answers.

This means, that when your prospects are looking for ways to improve the performance of their team, ways to increase their profits, ways to get more time back from themselves or whatever else you offer. More often than not the internet is one of their first points of call.

Your prospects are on the Internet right now looking for YOU and the solutions you offer. And if you're not in front of them, or they're going to your competitors' websites instead of yours; you're leaving profits and business revenue on the table!

If you're like most of the Coaches, Trainers and Consultants I speak to, you probably already have a website and know the importance of having an online presence in today's economy.

The problem is you haven't yet figured out how to make it work for you in your business.

Not long ago, I conducted a survey of over 4000 Coaches, Trainers and Consultants from across the world. And we discovered that over 99% of the people we asked were either not generating any online leads at all, or weren't generating as many as they would like.

In this section of the book we'll be looking at what the top 1% of Coaches, Trainers and Consultants who generate all the leads they can handle online do differently and how *you can do the same.*

How The Top 1% Of Coaches, Trainers and Consultants Use The Internet Differently

For the top 1% of Coaches, Trainers and Consultants the Internet is not just an information highway, it's a client attraction tool!

A client attraction tool that can be utilized 7 days a week, 24 hours a day and 365 days per year.

They don't care about having a fancy website with all the bells and whistles, all they care about is whether or not their website does what it's supposed to do.

Generate leads and convert them into clients.

Consider this:

- 1% of Coaches, Trainers and Consultants become wealthy in their lifetimes
- 4% become financially independent
- The other 95% accomplish neither
- That means 95% of Coaches, Trainers and Consultants are generally wrong.

However, if you want to be successful in life, simply do the opposite of what everyone else is doing. And guess what? It really works.

The tragedy of the 'Herd Mentality'

Earl Nightingale, in his famous audio program, *'The Strangest Secret'*, says the reason people fail is *conformity.*

The problem is that everyone is trying to act like everyone else, and with 95% of people not achieving worthwhile success; conformity is a sure-fire way to fail.

So while the majority of the Coaches, Trainers and Consultants are struggling to attract leads and clients from 9 to 5 Monday to Friday, the top 1% are able to attract leads and clients almost effortlessly, even while they sleep.

This is the Internet Marketing Revolution for the Coaches, Trainers and Consultants who are willing to look into it.

So How Do They Do It?

The burning question on your lips should be *"how?"*

How do the top 1% of Coaches, Trainers and Consultants use the Internet to attract clients and how can you do the same? And what are the implications for your personal income and your family security if you don't do this?

In just a minute you are about to get the answers to those questions. But first, it's important you understand the real purpose of your online activity.

What Is Internet Marketing All About Anyway?

The purpose of any Internet marketing campaign or anything you do online to win clients and earn more, comes down to two core principles:

1. *Increase the number of potential clients* who visit your website(s)

2. *Increase the percentage* of website visitors who convert into, coaching clients and increase your personal income

If any activity you engage in online, doesn't do either of those things then you're wasting your time.

The first rule is to STOP any activity that doesn't do these things immediately; such as, using your website as an online brochure to tell potential clients all about YOU, or pointless tweets and Facebook updates. These things do have their purposes and can be used effectively, but more often than not it's a complete waste of time.

So What Should You Be Doing To Increase Your Personal Income?

I've broken down everything you need to be doing online into five categories:

1. Traffic

2. Web conversion

3. Email follow up

4. Online and Offline Combination

5. Video

Traffic: Getting Your Potential Clients To Your Website

What Is Traffic?

When people say *"Traffic"* in relation to online marketing, it basically means attracting *visitors* to your website.

Getting traffic in of itself isn't difficult (in fact there are lots of ways to drive visitors to your websites, all of which can be implemented without too many headaches!) the difficult part is making sure the traffic you get to your site is qualified. You want quality not just quantity, and you only really want people who are looking for the service you offer to come to your site.

Some Of The Options For Driving Traffic.

✓ Email Marketing

✓ Direct Mail

- ✓ SEO (site Engine Optimization) Joint Ventures
- ✓ Referrals
- ✓ Social Media
- ✓ PR/Article Marketing
- ✓ PPC (Pay per click advertising) Display advertising
- ✓ Remarketing

As you can see, there are lots of ways to drive traffic to your website. The key is to use *multiple approaches* at the same time.

It may sound like basic common sense to use as many of these strategies to drive traffic as you can, but you would be surprised at how many Coaches, Trainers and Consultants don't do this as well as they should.

How many of these strategies do you currently have in place driving traffic to your website?

Web Conversion: Converting Website Visitors into Leads and Prospects

What is web conversion?

Web conversion means getting the visitors who come to your website to take the action you want them to take.

Once you've got visitors to visit your website, the next thing we need to do is convert that traffic into leads.

On a typical website, only 1% of visitors take any action at all. That means that for every 100 people you get to your website, only 1 of them will pick up the phone and call you, buy from you or take any action at all.

One of the things we need to be constantly improving with online marketing is your web conversion. We want as many people as possible to convert into a lead.

Passing The 8 Second Test: What Your Web Designer Won't Tell You

If you think about the way we 'surf' the web; we quickly go from one website to another never really staying too long and often never returning to the same site more than once.

In fact, the average time someone spends on any website is eight seconds.

You need to interrupt that pattern and get your prospects to stick to your website and take the action you want them to take.

So here is how you do that, by using the *AIDA Principle* (**A**ttention, **I**nterest, **D**esire and **A**ction)

Attention - The first thing we need to do is to get the attention of your prospects. This part of the AIDA formula is designed to stop your prospects in their tracks and get them to pay attention to what it is you have to say.

Interest - Then you get the potential clients interest.

Desire - Once you have their interest you then must create desire for the solution to their problem.

Action - And critically you must have a call to action.

What is it precisely that you want the reader to do upon reading your solution? If you don't tell them what to do they will not do anything and simply leave your site.

Using The Lead Conversion Model

The purpose of your site is not to get people to buy from you immediately. Even if you get everything right up to this stage, it's very unlikely someone is going to land on your website and immediately get the credit card out and buy.

The purpose of your website is to *begin a relationship with your prospects.*

Rather than using your website to sell your services begin the relationship by giving first.

What we are essentially saying to our prospects is this; *"you don't know me yet but I think I have something that's going to solve the problem you're having."*

This part forms the *'irresistible offer'* part of your marketing system as mentioned earlier.

Email follow Up: Turning A Luke Warm Prospect Into A Piping Hot Lead

Internet marketing doesn't just stop with your website. Once with got the traffic to convert into a lead that's just the beginning of the process.

The basic model is to give something of value away for free to generate the lead; get contact details and then develop a relationship over time, by using email.

Your website is there *to start the relationship*, the selling actually happens after that point.

In order for that lead to want to buy from you, you need to cultivate that relationship over time. That's where email marketing comes in.

If you're not emailing your prospects at least once per week you're almost certainly losing out on potential clients.

Don't be afraid to share details of your lives with potential clients. People buy from people and this helps build the relationship by showing that you're human.

Online and Offline Combination: The Death Of Cold calling

No matter how well online marketing is working for you, one of the biggest mistakes you can make is becoming solely dependent on the Internet. It's not safe for any Coaches,

Trainers and Consultants to have all his or her eggs in one basket, no matter how profitable that 'basket' may be. Combine your online follow up with one offline communications as well.

Some people will buy off the back of your online communication but some of your prospects will need the 'personal touch' before making that buying decision. This is where the use of direct mail and the telephone comes in. Don't move away from traditional marketing... Embrace it.

Video: The Next Website Revolution

In the past having video on your website was almost like a luxury. Something that was nice to have but not vital... Over the past few years that's been changing.

It is becoming increasingly important to include videos in your online marketing mix if you want to maximize the results you get from any element of your online marketing...

YouTube videos can be used to drive traffic to your website, the use of video on your webpages can help increase conversion and emailing videos to your leads can help improve the relationship and shorten lead time.

Did you know that YouTube is the second largest search engine after Google, not having a YouTube presence is a bit like not using a computer in your business, it can be done but you will lose out financially if you don't embrace new methods for growing your business.

Here's what we've covered during this chapter...

1. How the top % use the internet differently

2. Traffic

3. Web conversion

4. Email follow up

5. Online & offline combination

6. The next website revolution

Chapter 8
Premium Pricing For Profits And Premier Positioning

I thought it wrong to write this book on marketing without including at least a section dedicated to premium pricing and premier positioning.

Why? Well...

There are a number of reasons, but the main one is because I've noticed that so many Coaches, Trainers & Consultants are getting it so wrong; competing on price for scraps of business rather than hand picking the best clients.

It's pretty difficult to talk about one of these topics without talking about the other, because they go hand in hand.

You can't charge Premium Prices without getting your Positioning right. Otherwise, your potential clients simply wont buy and if you want to be positioned as a leader in the market, you're prices need to reflect it.

It's very rare that we come across something that is both the best and the cheapest, and when we do, it seems too good to be true, so we don't believe it anyway.

So the way you're 'Positioned', and your prices, are very important. It's something you need to get right in your business otherwise your profits will suffer.

I'm particularly excited about this subject and you should be too, because everything you'll discover can be instantly implemented to see an increase in profits and if an overnight increase in business profits doesn't excite you, I don't know what will!

There's a book called *'The Mayflower Madam'* by Sydney Biddle-Barrows. I've not yet read it myself but I've heard some very good things about the way the author ran her business.

Among other things, she gives an excellent demonstration of how Price and Positioning work hand-in-glove with each other.

In short, she ran an escort agency in New York. I think it was back in the late 1970s and early 1980s. Regardless of what you think about the morality of these things, she did some very savvy marketing.

In particular, she very expertly positioned herself in two very different ways:

1. At the top end of the market. (Charging a premium rate)

2. In the middle of the market. (Charging mid-range fees)

Nothing too clever in doing that.

But here's the clever part; the girls, the services they offered and even the switchboard operators were the same for *both* markets.

So why would someone pay top dollar for something they can get from the same place and for less money?

One word: *Positioning!*

The only difference in the two businesses was in the advertising and the prices. The advertising for the top end of the market involved very exclusive positioning.

Premier Positioning

Poisoning falls into three main categories;

1. Competitor Positioning:

Competitor positioning is how your competitors see you in the market. I wasn't even going to include this in this issue, but I think it's worth mentioning just to make you aware of the fact that it isn't worth you thinking about.

People spend far too much time wondering what their competitors are doing and what their competitors think, but quite frankly, what have your competitors got to do with anything?

If you want to be successful in business, you're going to have to do things your competitors won't like very much. In fact, if you're not annoying at least some of your competitors, you're probably not doing enough, and anyway who are they to decide how much you charge for your services, how you deliver your services or how much money you make?

Nobody! That's who. So I won't be mentioning them again and you shouldn't either. They are irrelevant!

2. Self-Positioning:

Self-positioning, is how you see yourself in the market. What do you think your services are worth?

Most Coaches, Trainers and Consultants come up with their prices in one of two ways;

1. They either pick a random number out of the sky and stick with it or...

2. More often than not they look at other people in their market, see what everyone else is charging, and pick a number somewhere between the lower and higher end

Let me tell you now the worst person to decide how much you should be charging for your services is you. It's difficult for you to value something you're so close to, and most of your competitors are under charging.

The best people to decide how much your services are worth, are your clients and there's no point asking them because they'll always give you a number lower than it really should be.

The only way to find out the true value of your services is to test it.

Every market has price elasticity, but more on that later.

3. Market Positioning:

Your market positioning is how your market see's you. Arguably the only one really worth paying any attention to and the best things about this is, you're in control.

It's entirely up to you as to how you want your market to see you and it's not for me to decide how that should be. But what I will say is this; someone has to be the leading player in your sector. Someone has to get all the best clients coming to them. Someone has to be the one who has the highest fees, the best service and the best business. Why shouldn't that someone be you?

Because if it's not you, it will be one of your competitors.

What Can You Do To Become A *'Key Person Of Influence'*, A Leading Player In Your Market – And Charge The Prices You Want?

So what is a *'Key Person of Influence'* anyway?

Every industry in any part of the world has *'Key People of Influence'*. Their names come up in conversation AND for all the right reasons.

They attract the best opportunities.

They are able to charge higher prices than their competitors and still win more business. They become almost like mini celebrities in their chosen field.

They enjoy a very special elite status because they are well connected, well known, well respected and very highly valued. They influence their industry rather than being influenced by it.

They don't work for the 'going rate' or work by the 'going terms', they work with whom they want, when they want and on their own terms.

Some people become a 'Key person of influence' almost by accident, it just sort of happens over time. But for most of us, this isn't the case and it's something we have to work at it.

The More Narrow Your Niche, The Broader Your Profits

It's a lot easier, smarter and profitable to be a big fish in a small pond, rather than a small fish in a big pond

As I mentioned earlier, almost every marketing expert, every marketing guru and every marketing specialist will say, *"to get the best results from your marketing, you need to niche."*

The truth is, you don't have to niche to make your marketing effective, but it certainly makes things easier. Especially if you want to become a 'key person of influence'.

In my experience, the Business/Executive Coaches that enjoy the most success, are those that have a well-defined niche and position themselves as the expert in that field.

There are just so many Business/Executive Coaches out there and there is far too much noise going on in the market place. So in order to be successful, you must differentiate yourself by making yourself stand out with a business that instantly grabs attention within that sector.

You see, once you have a well-defined niche, It's easier to market to that niche because your communication will be specific to their needs and not general where you are communicating to the whole business community.

Even the big brands such as Coca Cola and Ford Motors have defined niches that they market to. (The marketing for diet cola is typically aimed at the female market whereas coke zero is aimed at men, and Ford market each model of car to a different demographic e.g. large families, young adults, business professionals etc.)

When you're a Business/Executive Coach that has a niche, you literally eradicate the competition.

Think about it, there are thousands of Coaches, Trainers and Consultants, but only a *handful that specialise* in Accountancy, Retail, Technology etc. To become the leading player in the Accountancy sector will be a lot easier.

Become a big fish in a small pond, rather than a small fish in a big pond!

Getting The 'Expert' Status

To become a 'Key Person of influence' in your sector, you must be or at least be perceived as an expert in your chosen field.

I'm reminded of a quote I first heard from Dan Kennedy, the god-father of marketing;

"People are walking around with an umbilical cord in their hand looking for somewhere to plug it in".

Your market wants to be led.

And when they have problems that you can solve, they end up metaphorically knocking at your door and they are looking for reasons to believe in you. Even when they're sceptical and cynical, they still want to believe.

They want to believe you because if you're selling Coaching for Accountancy business owners' for example, it's reasonable for them to assume you're an expert on that. And the point is, if you've been specializing in your area for more than six months or so, you ARE an expert!

A great example of this predisposition and desire to be led and to believe, and one most of us can probably relate to, is the weight-loss industry. Most of us have at some time or other had excess weight to lose. I know I have.

It doesn't matter that we know intellectually that there are no short-cuts and no magic potions, but we all want to believe there is. We all want to believe there's a magic trick out there that can make us thinner, younger-looking, richer, and more attractive to the opposite sex. And we are predisposed to believe the guy or girl selling that solution, is an expert and knows his or her business.

That's why it's such a profitable industry.

So the first thing to understand about positioning yourself as the expert is: *people want to be led.*

The second thing to understand is *they want to believe.*

And the third thing, which is probably the hardest thing to get your head around is no one is ever going to appoint you as an expert unless you do it yourself.

Public Relations

So what do I mean when I say *'Public Relations'?*

I'm talking about your relationship with the public and more specifically your relationship with potential clients. No matter what business you're in, your reputation is key. What your potential clients think about you and how they see you is very important.

Public Relations is essentially managing this relationship with the public using the media. Rightly or wrongly, most people tend to believe what they read in magazines, hear on the radio and see on the television, we trust the media! Getting yourself and your business into the media can work wonders for your reputation.

If your potential clients see and hear you in the media, immediately you're seen as the expert.

Premium Pricing

As I said before, Premium Pricing and Premier Positioning go hand in hand. Just having high prices is a positioning statement in and of itself, but as you'll discover in a minute. There's a whole load more really cool stuff we can do with your pricing.

Pricing is one of the quickest and easiest ways to increase your business profits and in most cases, it's something you can do overnight and see an immediate effect.

And let's say your business turnover is £120K and as you'll see in a minute, a 10% increase in price isn't too much to ask and there are lots of ways you can do it without your clients ever really noticing.

Why charge more for what you do?

There are so many reasons for going down the Premium Pricing route, to a sane and rational person, it's not even a question of why, but when? But that's based on one assumption: *you're in possession of the facts.*

See, most Coaches, Trainers and Consultants view price-buying as a given. The idea everyone wants to pay the smallest price possible is so obvious it's rarely questioned. This is why most Coaches, Trainers and Consultants have the narrow approach to marketing and sales, as price-cutting and that promising they *"won't be beaten on price"* should do the job.

Let's imagine that I'm a business owner looking to grow my business by 10%.

What do you think I care about the most:

- ➤ Lowest Price?

- ➤ Getting the best possible Coach to help me exceed business targets, improve business performance and increase profits, which impacts how much cash I can take home each and every month?

I think I've made my point.

There are a few reasons Business/Executive Coaches DON'T want to raise their prices and they usually come down to one of three:

The Big Pricing Myths

Pricing Myth #1: The first big myth about pricing is *"You can't raise your prices without losing business".*

People seem to have this belief that raising your prices means losing business.

Well I can tell you now this isn't true. Think about it, I bet your weekly food shop doesn't cost the same as it did a year ago or even a month ago. I bet the cost of fuelling your car isn't the same as it was 6 months ago. I can give you millions of examples of this, the list is endless.

Here are the facts: In most parts of the world the value of money is decreasing, that, combined with inflation, means that if you're not raising your prices, you're actually losing money.

Pricing Myth #2: People buy based on price.

We know this isn't true because if it were, we would all drive around in the cheapest cars. Walk around in the cheapest clothes, and take our families on the cheapest holidays.

People don't buy on price, even though we sometimes like to think we do because it's the logical thing. The fact is, the majority of our buying decisions are based on *emotions.*

Our decisions are emotions based, we then use logic to justify the decision, it stops us feeling silly for spending a ridiculous amount of money on a new gadget or item of clothing.

Pricing Myth #3: If you're more expensive than your competitors, it gives them an edge.

Well we know this isn't true because if it were, car manufactures like Bentley and the other premium makes

125

would be struggling for business and we know that's not the case.

There are those who buy on the cheapest price (about 20% of the entire market). But the majority of the market doesn't. Even if they say they do.

There are those who enjoy spending more on what they buy, if it means they're getting better quality products/services or a better customer experience.

There are even those who won't buy something because it seems too cheap - myself included.

Being cheaper than your competitors doesn't give you the edge, you'll be going after a completely different audience. Think Virgin Atlantic VS, the typical budget airline.

Let your competitors fight with each other for those price buyers, while you target the VIP first class clients who want to spend more, buy more often and appreciate the true value of what you offer.

The Harsh Truth About 'Price Buyers'

If you think back to all the worst clients you ever had, I'll bet they all had something in common. I'll bet they all had the following two bad habits;

- ➤ They all pissed and moaned about price all the bloody time.
- ➤ They were always demanding more from you.

The thing is, price buyers don't just stop at low prices, in the same way a bully doesn't stop when they've hit you once. Price buyers gouge at you. Why they do this is a mystery to me and I'm not even going to pretend that I understand them. All I know is, I avoid them and let other people deal with them.

The second thing about price buyers is that they have no loyalty.

Why?

Because the moment someone offers a lower price, they'll take it. And someone will always offer a lower price because there's always someone willing to work for less money than you are.

And a third thing, price buyers are extremely slow to pay (if they ever pay at all). Often this is because they're just tight, plain and simple; but usually it's because they have no money.

So How Do You Charge More Without Losing Business?

The first way to increase your prices without losing business, is to simply raise your prices.

Sounds almost too simple doesn't it? The truth is, if you're like more than 80% of businesses out there, you're probably charging too little

Price Elasticity

In every business we have what is called Price Elasticity. Very basically 'Price Elasticity' means the amount you can raise your prices before you start to feel the strain from potential clients.

Studies have shown that you can probably raise your prices anywhere between 20-70% of what your charging now, without future clients really kicking up to much of a fuss. Makes you think doesn't it? What difference would it make to your business if you could increase your profits anywhere between 20-70%?

With each new client you bring on, try increasing the prices just a little, see if they notice any difference.

Example: If you currently charge £1000 (or your local currency equivalent) per month for you're coaching services. Your next clients would pay £1100, the client after that would pay £1200 and so on until you notice a big enough drop off in sales that you're happy to stay as you are.

If you raise your prices by 10%, but see a drop of in sales by

10% that's fine. Your still in profit and for less work. It's only IF you start to lose out that you stop and when I say *"stop"*, I don't mean stop raising your prices indefinitely, I mean stop, and try doing it another way by using one or all of the following strategies.

Make The Experience of Doing Business With You Extraordinary

One sure thing you can do that enables you to charge higher prices without losing business is to make the experience of doing business with you extraordinary and I'm not just talking about being different here, being different is simple and easy.

I'm talking about being better!

As I mentioned earlier, being better is also simple but not always easy, which is why so many businesses fail to jump this hurdle. So HOW exactly do you make the experience of doing business with you not just different, but better as well?

Quality: *This really should go without saying*

But I'll say it just in case it's something you're not already doing in your business, I'm going to make the assumption that you are great at what you do, so I won't spend too long on this, but if you're not as good as you should be at what you do, get better!

> *Quality is a very important element of making the experience of doing business with you extraordinary*

Reliability: *Do what you say you're going to do, when you say you're going to do it*

Sounds basic, but most businesses don't have the ability to stick to simple promises. People will pay more for a service they can count on.

Imagine you needed some work doing on your house. Would you rather pay more for someone who you know will turn up on time, clean up any mess they make and who gets the job done when they say they will, or pay less for someone who turns up late, is messy and doesn't stick to their time scale promises?

Make your business reliable and your clients will be willing to pay you your premium fees again and again

Consistency: *Being reliable once is all well and good but it all counts for nothing unless you can be reliable consistently*

How many times have you been to a shop, restaurant or bought a product or service that was good the first time round, but the next time you went there, they didn't live up to what you had expected?

Speed of Delivery (Short time scales): *Time is money!*

People will pay more to get things done in less time. Think next day delivery or express services, very easy to do and of course you can charge a premium for this.

The diamond encrusted version: *Offer the delux version*

One of the oldest tricks in the book when it comes to Premium Pricing, is to simply offer the 'diamond encrusted' or 'deluxe' version of what you offer.

So a potential client can either pay for your standard service OR go for the more expensive deluxe service, where they get all sorts of special treatment and bonuses. The best thing about it is this is something you can do straight away, as in right now! And it won't cost you anything to just have it there as an option.

Offering a deluxe version of your services has some secondary benefits as well, the main one being that it will make your standard service seem cheaper. You see, without contrast everything seems expensive, or cheap.

When you tell a potential client your price, a lot of the time they have nothing to compare it to, other than your competitors.

Telling them the price of the deluxe service first and then telling them the price of your standard service will soften the blow in their eyes and suddenly, instead of comparing your prices to your competitor. They're comparing your standard price to your deluxe offering.

Payment Plans

Offering a payment plan means rather than having to pay in a lump sum, giving your clients the opportunity to pay in instalments. This breaks down the investment to the minimum in the eyes of the buyer, making it easy for them to make a buying decision.

To some people, three monthly payments of £397.99 looks a lot more attractive, and seems a lot more affordable than one big payment of £1000, especially in businesses where cash flow is so important.

Offer Powerful Guarantees

Your potential clients want results. If they have a need for your services, but are still reluctant to buy. Having a compelling guarantee can get them to take that final step.

Giving a guarantee increases sales and reduces price-resistance because it takes away the risk for your potential clients.

This means two things:

1. Your potential clients get the warm and fuzzy feeling because they know if it doesn't work or you don't deliver what you say you will... Then they can get their money back!

2. It allows you to charge higher prices because there's no risk.

You know one of the best things about Premium Pricing and Premier Positioning?

The money?

Nope...

I won't deny it's nice to be paid more rather than being paid less and for doing more rewarding work in far better conditions. But that's not the best thing.

The best thing is the *quality of the people you get to deal with.*

I mean, I'm not what you would call a people person and I can and do go for days and even weeks without speaking to anyone other than my family and very close friends. But when I have to deal with people, it eases the pain mightily if they're pleasant, easy going and a joy to work with.

The thing is if you're doing business with people that you don't enjoy working with, two things are true:

1. It's your fault because you allowed them into your business and keep them there.

2. You don't have to put up with it.

If you do put up with it, then you're making a choice and If you don't want to put up it with it anymore you should fire them, plain and simple.

I remember the first time I fired one of my clients...

It's actually quite a liberating feeling, getting rid of those rotten apples. The thing with working with bad clients is they drain your time, they drain your energy, you don't like working with them and they probably even sense that you don't like working with them, and so they don't like working with you.

And on top of that because you're spending so much time and energy serving your bad clients, you have less time and energy left over to serve your good clients and so they suffer too, everyone loses!

The solution is simple; get rid of those bad clients and make it extremely difficult for them to ever do business with you again (that's where your positioning comes in).

I know that if you're like most Business/Executive Coaches, it may be a frightening thought to turn business away but trust me, it really isn't good for your business or your sanity to work with these people, they're like leeches on your profits.

I've made the mistake of working with bad clients before and so now, I'm extremely picky about whom I work with, I won't work with just anybody and you shouldn't either. You should have a very strict criteria and if your potential clients don't meet it show them the door.

Having a strict policy even has some side benefits as well; your potential clients will actually spend more time trying to convince you why you should let them work with you, rather than the other way around! More on that another time.

But for now, the message is very simple, *get rid of those bad apples*, in fact, go one step further and refer them to your biggest competitors!!

Here's what we've covered during this chapter...

1.   Competitor positioning

2.   Market positioning

3.   Self positioning

4.   Getting 'expert' status

5.   The big pricing myths

6.   The truth about price buyers

Chapter 9
Effective Time Management

*"What is important is seldom urgent and what is
urgent is seldom important."*
President Dwight D. Eisenhower

Have YOU got a minute?

Ever wonder what separates the very best of the best? Lots
of people would point to genetics, education, economic
climate, or the sector they operate in. But usually, those parts
aren't as big as you might think.

Imagine that 86,400 of your local currency is deposited into
your bank account. It's 100% legal and you're free to do
whatever you want with the money. The only catch is, at the
end of the day, whatever's left of the 86,400 gets taken away
from you and you lose out.

So what do you do? Well, anyone with an ounce of sanity would
make that most of every last penny! Wouldn't you?

Think about what you would do, if you had 86,400 to spend
each day.

So, what's the point?

Well every day you're given exactly 86,400 seconds. You can
do whatever you want with the time, but at the end of the day,
whatever time you've not made the most of gets taken away
from you and you never get it back. The thing about us humans
is *we're procrastinators!*

We put things off and we put things off some more, until it
eventually gets to the point where we have nothing more to

put off other than 'putting things off' itself. The big frustration isn't 'not knowing what the solution is', it's the 'not getting round to doing it' that holds most of us back.

In my opinion there is no such thing as time management; to be effective you must manage yourself.

Below will help you calculate what your time is worth:

Target Income	⇨	**A**
Working days in a year	⇨	235
Hours in a working day	⇨	**C** 7
Working hours in a year	⇨	**D** 1645

A /D = Your hourly worth (before deductions) ⇨ **E**

Doing this exercise will really help put your time into perspective. It's also worth considering that the average person is effective for between 25 minutes to four hours per day.

Most Coaches, Trainers and Consultants have no idea where the time goes. This in turn leads to frustration as you can spend ten to twelve hours a day working, yet feel as if you haven't achieved much. Being reactive often causes this.

Common causes of this are:
- Your email
- Clients calling you unexpectedly
- Your mobile phone
- Unplanned meetings
- YOU
- Internet
- Social media.

How to overcome this:

You now know what your time is worth in hard cash, and you have identified the time thieves. So, now what?

A Time Audit

For the next ten days, be absolutely honest with yourself and record exactly where you spend your time by keeping a time audit. In this audit, include every single thing that you do, including travelling, looking up the sports results on the web and the time you spend on Facebook.

Below is an example of what your time audit sheet could look like.

TIME AUDIT SHEET		
Time	Activity	Enough/not enough time?
8:00 - 8:30		
8:30 - 9:00		
9:00 - 9:30		
9:30 - 10:00		
10:00 - 10:30		
10:30 - 11:00		
11:00 - 11:30		
11:30 - 12:00		
12:00 - 12:30		
12:30 - 1:00		
1:00 - 1:30		
1:30 - 2:00		
2:00 - 2:30		
2:30 - 3:00		
3:00 - 3:30		
3:30 - 4:00		
4:00 - 4:30		
4:30 - 5:00		

Time Analysis

Upon completion of the above audit, identify where if you're spending too much, or perhaps too little time on tasks.

Then answer these questions:

- When are you most productive?
- What do you do most every day that will take you closer to achieving your goal?
- Does your analysis reflect that?
- If you had more time what would you do?
- If you had less time what would you do?
- In what areas of your life is procrastination a problem for you?

Strategies used by the Top Coaches, Trainers and Consultants

Having a well-defined goal

By having a well-defined goal you know exactly where you and your business are going and what precisely you must do to get there. This helps you prioritize what needs to be done. A question to ask is 'what 3 things must I do today that will take me closer to my goal?' Once your priorities have been established you'll have the clarity. Remember this doesn't only apply to your business life but also to your personal life

Delegation

The only way you'll get everything done, is by delegating that task that can be delegated, this applies to the Coaching, Training and Consultancy owner with a team of 100 and the sole trader.

There are numerous tasks that can be outsourced:

✓ Outsourcing/Virtual admin support

www.odesk.com/-

www.elance.com/

www.freelancer.com/work/market-research-india/

www.peopleperhour.com/freelance/ virtual+pa+lifestyle+assistant

www.talentgurus.net/virtual-assistant.html

Discover the secret to saying NO!

It really easy to get into the habit of saying yes to everything. An example of this is: The client that gives you a lot of business then asks you to fill a role that you have no expertise or experience in. You believe it is better to say yes rather than let your competitors do it. That's so wrong.

The top firms have a well-defined goal and know how they're going to get there. If they're asked to do something that will not take them closer to their goal then the answer is a resounding NO!

Create a Timeline

Once you have decided on what needs to be done, set a timeline. A goal without a timeline is a 'wish' so schedule time for everything:

- Contacting clients

- Writing proposals

- Following up on leads

- Internal/external meetings

- Admin.
- Creating to-do list
- Family time.
- Etc

Make a Decision

The most successful Coaches, Trainers and Consultants have the ability to make a decision. It has been found that indecisiveness creates stress for the person that's being indecisive. Clearly communicate your expectations to your team.

One of the biggest time robbers is 'miscommunication'. Whenever you say or think 'I didn't mean it like that,' this is a sign you haven't communicated your expectations clearly and precisely.

There is no such thing as an inflexible client, friend, or partner, just an inflexible communicator

If you were to accept that presumption then you would take responsibility for the outcome, and it gets you to look at your communication style.

Just some of the benefits of systemizing your business;

- ✓ More time
- ✓ More money
- ✓ Business works if you're there or not
- ✓ More valuable – a business with documented workable systems is worth far more than a business that has no systems
- ✓ Easier to take your business to the next level – franchise, license, public float or sell.

Systemize every aspect of your business

As mentioned before, management is closely linked to effective communications. Numerous studies have shown that the most successful Coaches, Trainers & Consultants systemize every single aspect of their business.

A good example of this is McDonalds Restaurants;

Whatever your personal opinion of them, you know that wherever in the world you are, when visiting a McDonalds, the food and the service is consistent

The reason is quite simple; everything is systemized. From the way you're greeted to how the staff always 'up sell you' to the larger size, to the fact that regardless of what the temperature is outside you're always given ice whether you ask for it or not (this, by the way, saves McDonalds millions of dollars every year).

Imagine if your Coaching, Training and Consultancy business could run without you being there? That's what systems can do for your business. Every member of staff knows exactly what they need to do and when, and every task is handled the same way, cutting down on problems.

Systemizing your business will give you a very good idea of the flow of information or activity within your business. It allows you, the owner to go on holidays and know everything will be done as it should be. When new people join your team there will be a manual they can follow. There will be consistency in all activities.

Systemizing your business can be as simple as documenting all daily, weekly or monthly activities each employee needs to do. This can be done by writing them down, or possibly photographing, or capturing them on video or audio CD.

Obviously there are elements that you have learned about that you may want to give more thought to or find out more information on. Here though to start the ball rolling is something that you can implement straight away!

Action Steps

- Sit down with your team, and come up with a way to start documenting what they do. Then start to compile it into a 'Systems' folder.

- Create a Time Audit sheet and fill it out.

- Get everyone into the habit of documenting even the smallest things, from how to answer the telephone, to how to follow up a client.

- Get someone to collate all of the information and keep it in one place, then regularly update it.

Here's what we've covered during this chapter...

1. Time audit

2. Time analysis

3. Delegation

4. Saying "NO!"

Conclusion

First I want to say a big thank you for investing the time into reading this book. I hope you've found it useful.

The big tragedy is that you may be better than the competition. In fact, you may be the best Coach, Trainer or Consultant in the world. Unfortunately, that's not enough to be successful. To succeed you must know how to Market effectively.

The irony is that your competitors or other professionals in your field can have an inferior service to yours, but if they are better Marketers, they will undoubtedly take your business.

The truth is, that for you to be successful as a Coach, Trainer or Consultant in today's economy, you absolutely must be excellent at Marketing.

Occasionally, I'll meet Coaches, Trainers and Consultants who are broke or don't have as much money as they would like, who aren't generating enough leads, who are desperate for more clients and who say that they're willing to do "whatever it takes" to turn things around.

But when you look at their behaviour and lack of actions it tells a completely different story.

There's no shame in being broke or not having enough clients... the only thing to be ashamed of is not doing anything about it!

If you're not yet generating enough leads in your business or you're frustrated with the clients you keep missing out on, - the information you have read in the book has the power to help you begin to turn things around. *But if, and only if you actually use it!*

About the Author

Drew Edwards is the worlds leading Marketing and Client Attraction expert for Coaches, Trainers & Consultants. He has personally helped more than 1,000 Coaches, Trainers & Consultants generate more leads and attract more clients. In addition to his coaching and writing, Drew is also a specialist keynote speaker for the Coaching, Training & Consultancy Industry.

Very rarely does he open up his private client list to new clients, and the ones he has, very rarely leave!

Having written numerous eBooks, and a number of home study courses for the industry including *'The Elite Client Attraction System'*, *'The Coaches, Trainers & Consultants Profit-Club'*. He is also the creator of the www.eliteclientattraction.com/marketingacademy/ which is one of the world's leading client attraction resources for Coaches, Trainers and Consultants.

Acknowledgements

Firstly, a big thanks to my Mum, Valerie, who has always been there for me and provided unlimited love, support and guidance. My Dad, Terry, who has been a constant inspiration throughout my life and now works closely with me in the business.

Over the years I have read many books by some of the leaders of the marketing and self-development industry too many to mention here, but a special thanks to; Dan Kennedy and all his books, Jon McCulloch, Chris Cardell, Peter Thomson, Anthony Robbins, Brian Tracey, Zig Ziglar, Robert Skrobb, Chet Holmes, Michael Gerber, Stephen Covey and Seth Godin.

And finally, special thanks to Alexa Whitten (my book writing coach) for not giving up on me.